Intermediate Commercial Correspondence

中级商务信函

[德] David Clarke 原著
李相敏 吕和 张晓武 编译

北京大学出版社
PEKING UNIVERSITY PRESS

著作权合同登记　图字：01-2008-3243

图书在版编目（CIP）数据

中级商务信函 /（德）克拉克（Clarke,D.）原著；李相敏等编译. —北京：北京大学出版社，2009.3

（全国职业技能英语系列教材）

ISBN 978-7-301-14966-9

Ⅰ. 中…　Ⅱ. ①克… ②李…　Ⅲ. 商务-英语-信函-写作-职业教育-教材　Ⅳ. H315

中国版本图书馆 CIP 数据核字（2009）第 023035 号

书　　名：中级商务信函

著作责任者：〔德〕克拉克（Clarke,D.）　原著　李相敏　等编译

责 任 编 辑：张建民

标 准 书 号：ISBN 978-7-301-14966-9/H·2207

出 版 发 行：北京大学出版社

地　　址：北京市海淀区成府路 205 号　100871

网　　址：http://www.pup.cn

电　　话：邮购部 62752015　发行部 62750672　编辑部 62755217　出版部 62754962

电 子 邮 箱：zbing@pup.pku.edu.cn

印　刷　者：北京宏伟双华印刷有限公司

经　销　者：新华书店

787 毫米×1092 毫米　16 开本　10 印张　260 千字

2009 年 3 月第 1 版　2009 年 3 月第 1 次印刷

定　　价：28.00 元（配有光盘）

全国职业技能英语系列教材

编委会

总 序

我国高职高专教育的春天来到了。随着国家对高职高专教育重视程度的加深,职业技能教材体系的建设成为了当务之急。高职高专过去沿用和压缩大学本科教材的时代一去不复返了。

语言学家 Harmer 指出:“如果我们希望学生学到的语言是在真实生活中能够使用的语言,那么在教材编写中接受技能和产出技能的培养也应该像在生活中那样有机地结合在一起。”

教改的关键在教师,教师的关键在教材,教材的关键在理念。我们依据《高职高专教育英语课程教学基本要求》的精神,秉承“实用为主,够用为度,学以致用,触类旁通”的原则,历经两年艰辛,为高职高专学生编写了这套专业技能课和实训课的英语教材。

本套教材的内容贴近工作岗位,突出岗位情景英语,是一套职场英语教材,具有很强的实用性、仿真性、职业性,其特色体现在以下几个方面:

1. 开放性

本套教材在坚持编写理念、原则及体例的前提下,不断增加新的行业或岗位技能英语分册作为教材的延续。

2. 国际性

本套教材以国内自编为主,以国外引进为辅,取长补短,浑然一体。目前已从德国引进了某些行业的技能英语教材,还将从德国或他国引进优秀教材经过本土化后奉献给广大师生。

3. 职业性

本套教材是由高职院校教师与行业专家针对具体工作岗位、情景过程共同设计编写。同时注重与行业资格证书相结合。

4. 任务性

基于完成某岗位工作任务而需要的英语知识和技能是本套教材的由来与初衷。因此,各分册均以任务型练习为主。

5. 实用性

本教材注重基础词汇的复习和专业词汇的补充。适合于在校最后一学期的英语教学，着重培养和训练学生初步具有与其日后职业生涯所必需的英语交际能力。

本教材在编写过程中，参考和引用了国内外作者的相关资料，得到了北京大学出版社外语编辑部的倾力奉献，在此，一并向他们表示敬意和感谢。由于本套教材是一种创新和尝试，书中瑕疵必定不少，敬请指正。

丁国声
教育部高职高专英语类专业教学指导委员会委员
河北省高校外语教学研究会副会长
河北外国语职业学院院长
2008年6月

Contents

1 Form and layout of business letters

What is a business letter?

- Business letters—and facsimile messages ('faxes') and emails—are written by one firm, organization or individual to another about business matters. The writer of the letter etc is the **sender**; the receiver is the **addressee**.
- A **fax** is a business letter that is sent electronically, usually down a phone line. Although the layout may be different, the style of faxes is the same as that of business letters.
- An **email** is more like a spoken message in written form. For this reason, emails tend to make use of short forms (*didn't, he's, they've*) and a more conversational style, for example, *This is to let you know that the goods arrived here safely today*, instead of the more formal, *This is to confirm that the goods were safely delivered to our premises today.*
- The **aim** of routine business letters and faxes is to...

...give the addressee information:	*The goods left ourstores on 15 May.*
...ask the addressee for information:	*When did the goods leave your stores?*
...ask the addressee to do something:	*Please confirm receipt of this order.*

- When you write to a firm for the first time, say **who** you are, **where** you got the firm's address from and **what** you want the addressee to do. If you are writing to a firm you already know, just say **why** you are writing and **what** you want.

Always obey the **ABC Rule** when you write a business letter, fax or email:

A Be **accurate.** Make sure that all details, i.e. names, dates, references, order numbers, prices etc, are correct and complete.

B Be **brief,** Say what you want to say and then stop. Always keep strictly to the point.

C Be **clear.** Use plain, simple English. Never use unnecessarily technical language or 'jargon'. Write in an easy, natural style without being either too formal or too familiar. However, use **long forms**, e.g. *they are, he did not, they would be*, in business correspondence.

A Model letter

Ahrens & Kessler GmbHin Bremen is a wholesale supplier of outdoor clothing and footwear. In this enquiry, Karin Feldmann in Purchasing asks Robert Carr & Co Ltd, a British manufacturer of wax coats and jackets, to send her their latest catalogue.

ahrens & kessler GmbH
Dieselstrabe 24 Tel. +49–(0)421–15 26 37 Internet www.ahrens–kessler.de
D–28217 Bremen Fax +49–(0)421–15 26 38 E-mail info@ahrens–kessler.de — a

Robert Carr & Co Ltd
18 Oldham Street
Bradford
BD4 7KL
England — b

26 January 20.. — c

Your ref:
Our ref: KF/sl — d

Enquiry about outdoor clothing — e

Dear Sir or Madam ← f

As you will see from the enclosed image brochure, we are a leading German distributor of outdoor clothing and footwear.

Further to your advertisement in the winter edition of *Leisure World*, we would be greatful if you could send us three copies each of your current catalogue and price-lists. We are particularly interested in your Carlton range of waxed coats and jackets. ← g

Thank you for your trouble and we look forward to hearing from you soon.

Yours faithfully ← h

Ahrens & Kessler GmbH

Karin Feldmann ← i

Karin Feldmann
Purchasing

CC Markus Redwitz, Marketing ← j

Enc image brochure ← k

a **Are these statements true, false or you can't say because of lack of information? Correct the false statements.**

1 The letter is addressed to Ahrens &Kessler in Bremen.
2 The letter was signed by Karin Feldmann.
3 Karin is Ahrens & Kessler's purchasing manager.
4 The image brochure is in four clours.
5 Ahrens & Kessler is particularly interested in footwear.
6 Robert Carr & Co advertised in *Leisure world.*

b **Look at parts a-k of the letter again. Match them with the terms 1-11 below.**

1 complimentary close
2 copy circulated / carbon copy
3 date
7 body of letter
8 reference
9 salutation

4 enclosures
5 inside address
6 letterhead
10 signature block
11 subject line

c **Turn the letter below into a more informal e-mail by replacing the underlined words and expressions with items from the box.**

advert	attached PDF document	Best wishes	Good morning
let us have	seller	Thanks a lot	we'd be glad
We're especially keen on	we're	you'll	latest

Dear Sir or Madam[1]

As you will[2] see from the enclosed image brochure[3], we are[4] a leading German distributor[5] of outdoor clothing and footwear.

Further to your advertisement[6] in the winter edition of Leisure World, we would be grateful[7] if you could send us[8] three copies each of your current[9] catalogue and price-lists. We are particularly interested in[10] your Carlton range of waxed coats and jackets.

Thank you[11] for your trouble and we look forward to hearing from you soon.

Yours faithfully[12]

Karin Feldmann

B Notes on business letters

1 Format and layout

There is no standard format or layout for business letters in English, so you can use the German DIN-form if you prefer.

However, in modern business correspondence, the **American block form** has become almost standard practice throughout the English-speaking world. Here the parts are simply listed one after the other on the left. In this book, we have used the American block form throughout.

Note that in the block form, **no commas** are used in addresses (b), at the end of the subject line (e), and after the salutation and complimentary close (f,h). This is called 'open punctuation'. In the body of the letter, normal punctuation is used.

2 Letterhead (a)

As there are no fixed 'rules' about company letterheads in the English-speaking world, they vary widely from one company to another. However, they always show **a**) the company's registered name and address, and perhaps its registration number, **b**) its telephone and fax numbers and **c**) almost always its e-mail and/or website addresses. Note that when answering a letter, the inside address (see below) of your letter must always be exactly the same as the letterhead of the original letter.

3 Inside address(b)

The inside address shows who the letter is to, i.e. the name and address of the addressee. If you are not using a window envelope, make sure that the address on the envelope is exactly the same as the inside address. If you are replying to a letter, always copy the inside address from the letterhead of the original letter (see **2** above).

Look at these examples of British and American addresses.

UK

Outside London

Anglian Freight Co Ltd	no point after **Co** (Company) and **Ltd** (Limited)
12 Essex Road	building number before street name
Ipswich	postal town alone
IP49HJ	postcode alone
United Kingdom	name of country, i.e. United Kingdom

London addresses

London Insurance Co Ltd	no point after **Co** (Company) and **Ltd** (Limited)
38 Vienna Gardens	building number before street name
London SW17GH	London+space+postcode; no country with London addresses

USA

Western Electronics Inc.	point after Inc. (Incorporated)
182 Edison Avenue	building number before street name
Dallas, TX 76432	comma + space between postal town and ZIP code
U.S.A.	U.S.A. 'closed', i.e. with points

Always use the official two-letter abbreviations for US states—e.g. **TX** for **Texas**—in ZIP-codes. This is important because the US Postal Service does not guarantee delivery of mail with incorrect codes.

ZIP code abbreviations of names of US states

Alabama	AL	Kentucky	KY	North Dakota	ND
Alaska	AK	Louisiana	LA	Ohio	OH
Arizona	AZ	Maine	ME	Oklahoma	OK
Arkansas	AR	Maryland	MD	Oregon	OR
California	CA	Massachusetts	MA	Pennsylvania	PA
Colorado	CO	Michigan	MI	Rhode Island	RI
Connecticut	CT	Minnesota	MN	South Carolina	SC
Delaware	DE	Mississippi	MS	South Dakota	SD
District of Columbia	DC	Missouri	MO	Tennessee	TN
Florida	FL	Montana	MT	Texas	TX
Georgia	GA	Nebraska	NE	Urah	UT
Hawaii	HI	Nevada	NV	Vermont	VI
Idaho	ID	New Hampshire	NH	Virginia	VA
Illinois	IL	New Jersey	NJ	Washington	WA
Indiana	IN	New Mexico	NM	West Virginia	WV
Iowa	IA	New YorK	NY	Wisconsin	WI
Kansas	KS	North Carolina	NC	Wyoming	WY

Universal Postal Union

The **Universal Postal Union** is a division of the United Nations. Go to its website at www.upu.int to find out how to write addresses in over 180 countries.

On the UPU's **homepage**, click **Addressing** in the **Resources** menu, and then **Postal Addressing Systems in Member Countries** in the **Addressing** menu. Then scroll to the country you want and click **Display.**

4 **Date** (c)

There is no standard way of writing the date in English. In **general usage**, all the following forms are acceptable, though forms with the **day after the month** are more common in the USA:

12th April 2005	ordinal number—month—year
12 April 2005	cardinal number—month—year

April 12th, 2005 month—ordinal number + comma—year
April 12, 2005 month—cardinal number + comma—year

However, 12 April 2005 is by far the most common form in modern business usage.

Be careful with 'all-number dates' like 11.6.04, 11/6/04 and 11-6-04. In Europe these mean 11 June 2004, but in North America and some Asian countries, including Japan, they mean 6 November 2004.

For this reason, it is best to avoid all-number dates in external business letters and documents, although you can use them in internal notes and memos, and in private correspondence.

5 **Reference** (d)

When answering a business letter, always give the reference of the original letter under **Your ref:** and your own reference under **Our ref:**.

References normally show **a**) who wrote the letter and **b**) who typed it. However, they may also give other details, such as the date or an identity number. The writer's initials come first, usually in capitals, followed by the typist's initials in small letters, for example **KF/sl** (see model letter).

6 **Salutation** (e)

If you know the name of the person who will deal with your letter, then use it, for example, **Dear Ms Carter** or **Dear Mr Hammond.** If you normally use the other person's first name, then use it in business communications as well, for example, **Dear Helen** or **Dear Jim.**

Note that the neutral form **Ms** [miz:] is the standard form of address for women in business situations. This is because the traditional forms **Miss** (for unmarried women) and **Mrs** (for married, divorced or widowed women) depend on a woman's marital status, i.e. on her relationship to a man. This dependence is thought inappropriate in modern usage. If you don't know the person's name, use the impersonal form **Dear Sir or Madam**. In some American and Canadian letters, you may see **Ladies and Gentlemen:**, or even **Gentlemen:**, but in normal business usage this salutation is now going out of use.

Note that in the American and Canadian form **Mr., Mrs., Ms.** And the academic title **Dr.** are written with a point, but in the British form they are 'open' (**Mr, Mrs, Ms, Dr**).

7 **Subject line** (f)

The subject line says what the letter is about in as few words as possible. It is usually written **in bold** or underlined, for example, **Enquiry about outdoor clothes** or Enquiry about outdoor clothes. In the American form, the subject line may start with the word **Subject:**, but this is unusual in British usage.

Note that the **subject line** can come before or after the salutation according to company practice. However, if in doubt, position it **before** the salutation as in the model letter on page 3.

8 **Body of letter** (g)

The text of a business letter is called 'body'.

To help the reader, when you write the body of a business letter, always use one paragraph for each point and leave a space ('white line') between each paragraph.

9 **Complimentary close** (h)

Always finish your letter with a complimentary close. You can choose the most appropriate formulation from the following table.

UK and Commonwealth except Canada

	Salutation	**Complimentary close**	**Formality**
Impersonal	Dear Sir or Madam	Yours faithfully	formal
Personal	Dear Lisa	Yours	friendly
		Yours sincerely	quite formal
	Dear Mr Cobb	Yours sincerely	neutral

USA and Canada

	Salutation	**Complimentary close**	**Formality**
Impersonal	Dear Sir or Madam	Yours truly	formal
	Ladies and Gentlemen	Truly yours	
		Very truly yours	
Personal	Dear Nick	Yours	friendly
		Sincerely yours	neutral
		Yours sincerely	quite formal
	Dear Ms. Harper	Sincerely yours	neutral
		Yours sincerely	

If you know the other person very well, you can use **With best/kind regards** or **With best wishes.**

10 Signature block (i)

In the **signature block**, the name of the company often comes above the writer's signature, and his or her position within the company below it.

If the letter is signed by some body other than the writer, then this must be made clear by putting **for** or, more formally, **on behalf of** immediately before the writer's name below the signature, for example:

Yours faithfully
Robert Carr & Company Limited

Peter Edwards

For/On behalf of Helen Shaw
Sales Manager

11 Copies (j)

The letters **cc** originally stood for **carbon copy/copies.** However, 'cc' also stands for **copy/copies circulated**, which has been suggested as a sensible modern alternative. After all, nowadays there are no 'carbon copies'.

If the sender does not want the addressee to know that other people have been sent copies of the letter, then **bcc** for **blind copy/copies circulated** is put onto the **file copy** of the letter (for example: **bcc** Jonathan Barker, Legal Department).

12 Enclosures (k)

If you put something into the envelope with the letter, then say so under **Enc** (or **Encl**) for one item or **Encs** (or **Encls**) for two or more items.

C Practising Language

1 Write out these abbreviations in full.

1 bcc	*blind copy circulated*	**6** encls	...
2 cc	...	**7** fax	...
3 Co	...	**8** Ltd	...
4 email	...	**9** tel	...
5 enc	...		

2 There are two mistakes in each of these addresses. Find the mistakes and correct them.

a Aubade Automotive Parts Ltd
Rose Lane 47
Norwich, NR17UH
England

b United Oil Inc.
267, Delaware Road
TX67432, Dallas
U.S.A.

c Thomas Low Ltd.
45 Surrey Docks
London
E18HJ

d Union Bank of Scotland PLC
12 Balmoral Square,
Inverness
Scotland
IN2 8DS

e Ms. Laurie Bond,
438 Ocean Boulevard
Los Angeles
CA 62371
U.S.A.

3 Write out these dates and then read them out to your partner. Look at the example first.

EAMPLE: 19.11.02 write: *19 Novermber 2002*
Say: the nineteenth of November, two thousand (and) two

1 25.4.92 ...
2 7.12.00 ...
3 15.2.02 ...
4 5.3.03 ...
5 10.08.38 ...
6 31.01.01 ...

4 You have received a record of deliveries with all-number dates from a Japanese supplier. Write out the dates in a European form. Don't forget that in these dates, the month comes before the day.

1 11/03/00 *3 Novermber 2000*
2 01/05/01 ...
3 08/09/02 ...
4 05/08/03 ...

5 Use the numbers 1-4 to link the salutations to a suitable complimentary close, a-d. In one case, more than one solution is possible.

1 Dear Sir or Madam	**a** Yours
2 Dear Martin	**b** Yours sincerely
3 Ladies and Gentlemen	**c** Yours faithfully
4 Dear Ms Adams	**d** Very truly yours

6 This letter from Robert Carr & Co Ltd to Ahrens & Kessler GmbH is complete, but the parts are in the wrong order. Write out the complete letter in the correct order.

a
Ahrens & Kessler GmbH
DieselstraBe 24
D-28217 Bremen

b 4 February 2..

c cc: John Garner, Export Planning

d Dear Ms Feldman

e

f Encs: catalogue(3x), prece-list(3x)

g European Sales

h Your enquiry of 16 February

i Ranchit Patel

j Your ref: KF/sl

k Our ref: JB/bb

l Yours sincerely

m
Thank you very much for your enquiry of 26 January .
We are happy to send you the catalogues and price-lists you asked for, including details of our Carlton range of waxed outer clothing.
We hope that you find our products of interest and would be delighted to hear from you again.

2 Office communication: telephoning

Model phone calls: asking to speak to somebody; arranging appointments

Useful phrases: asking to speak to somebody (phoning somebody, answering the phone, putting a caller through, saying somebody is not available, offering help, asking for information, getting out of trouble, saying goodbye); arranging appointments (asking for an appointment, fixing a time and date, accepting and rejecting suggestions, closing)

Telephoning in business

In spite of the huge increase in electronic mailing in the form of emails, text messaging and faxes, it is hard to exaggerate the importance of telephoning in business.

Telephoning is the main means of communication in countless situations, both as **internal calls** within the same company and as **external calls** with customers and suppliers. In an increasingly global economy, a large number of external calls are carried out in English, which is now the common language of international business.

Routine telephone calls

This section introduces you to the language you need to make routine telephone calls in these basic business situations:

1 Calling a person in his or her office.
2 Leaving a message.
3 Making appointments and arranging visits.

The situation

Sam Kavanagh is an Irish manufacturer of quality outdoor clothing. Sam wants to market his Stormy Weather range of products in Germany, so he asks the German Embassy in Dublin for advice. The embassy gives Sam the names of some specialist German marketing organisations that help companies to sell their products in Germany.

Sam's first choice is UB Consult GmbH, a fashion consultancy in Düsseldorf. Sam chooses this firm because UB Consult is very experienced, and has good contacts to the Netherlands and Scandinavia as well. He also likes the idea of dealing directly with the joint owners, Uwe Bach and his wife Ulla.

A Taking notes

2 1 **Makine and answering calls**

In this dialogue, Sam Kavanagh is calling Ulla Bach of UB Consult for the first time. Unfortunately, Ulla is not in her office so the person taking the call, Ulla 's secretary,Lisa Schmitz, asks if she can take a message.

a **You are Lisa. Listen to the dialogue and note down the following information.**

1 Who is calling?
2 What does the caller want?
3 What does the caller want Lisa to do?
4 What is the caller's phone number?
5 Why is the message 'quite urgent'?

b **Listen again and note down who or what the pronouns in *italics* refer to. Look at the example first.**

EXAMPLE Do *you* mind if *I* speak English?
'You' is Lisa, and 'I' is Sam.

1 Could *you* spell that for *me*, please?
2 *Yes, that's* right, but *we* don't pronounce *them.*
3 *She* had to go out, *I'*m afraid.
4 Can *you* ask her to ring *me*, please?
5 Could *you* tell *her it's* quite urgent?
6 *I'*ll make sure *she* has *your* message as soon as *she* gets back.

(3) 2 Arranging appointments

In this dialogue, Sam Kavanagh's secretary, Kate Connors, is calling Lisa Schmitz to arrange an appointment for her boss to meet the Bachs at the ispo Sportmode fair in Munich, which they are all attending. Note the use of first names, which is usual in the English-speaking world.

a Listen to the phone conversation and complete Lisa's email to Kate with the missing details.

From: Lisa Schmitz<lisa.schmitz@ubconsult.de>
To: <k.connors@kavanaghoutdoor.ie>
Sent: Tue, 18 Jan 05 11:17:49
Subject: Arrangements for meeting
Cc: Uwe Bach <uwe.bach@ubconsult.de>

Hi Kate

I thought I'd just *confirm*[1] the arrangements we made for Mr Kavanagh's...[2] with Mr and Mrs Bach at the ispo...[3] fair in Munich next...[4], as follows:

Time/date ...[5] am on Saturday,1...[6]
Place Room...[7], first...[8], small...[9], ...[10] entrance.

All the best

Lisa

b Put in the missing prepositions. Then check your answers by listening to the phone conversation again. Not all the answers are in the conversation.

1 What can I do... you?
2 Sam and the Bachs are meeting...[1] a fair...[2] Munich...[3] February.
3 They want to meet...[1] the first day...[2] the fair.
4 Uwe Bach has booked a room...[1] the small conference centre...[2] Saturday morning.
5 The conference centre is...[1] the Theresienhöhe entrance...[2] the exhibition ground.
6 The room...[1] which the meeting is taking place is...[2] the first floor...[3] the conference centre.

B Telephoning language

1 Making and answering calls

Phoning somebody

My name's... Can/Could/May I speak to Mr/Ms..., please?

Can/Could/May I speak to somebody in purchasing/sales/accounts/..., please?

Can/Could/May I speak to whoever is in charge of/responsible for marketing/sales/..., please?

Good morning	00:00 to 12:00
Good afternoon	12:00 to 18:00
Good evening	18:00 to 24:00

Note that in ordinary English **good day** is no longer used as a greeting.

Answering the phone

Good morning/afternoon....

Can I help you/How can I help you?

Who's calling/May I have your name, please?

Putting a caller through

Can/Could you hold the line, please?

I'll put you through to export/to...

Just one moment, please. I'll see if... is available/free.

Saying somebody is not available

I'm sorry, but... is not available/free at the moment.

I'm afraid... is not at his/her desk/not in his/her office at present.

I'm sorry, but... is away/out of the office today.

I'm sorry, but... is in a meeting at the moment.

I'm afraid that... is at lunch/on holiday.

I'm sorry, but... is speaking on another line at present.

Offering help

Can I take a message for... ?

Would you like to call back, or should ...call you?

Would you like to leave a message?

I'll ask... to call you back as soon as possible.

Can I put you through to his/her assistant/secretary?

Asking for information

What was the name again, please?

Could you spell that for me, please?

The English alphabet and international spelling code

A	Alpha	I	India	Q	Quebec	Y	Yankee
B	Bravo	J	Juliette	R	Romeo	Z	Zulu
C	Charlie	K	Kilo	S	Sierra		
D	Delta	L	Lima	T	Tango		
E	Echo	M	Mike	U	Uniform		
F	Foxtrot	N	November	V	Victor		
G	Golf	O	Oscar	W	Whisky		
H	Hotel	P	Papa	X	X-ray		

('Z' is pronounced 'zed' in British English and 'zee' in American English.)

Can/could you give me your fax/phone/mobile phone number, please?

Saying phone numbers

- Say the individual numbers one after the other. Say the number **0** as the letter **o** (common in British English) or **zero** (common in American and International English).

- **Never** use tens, eg 'fifty-seven' for 'five-seven'.
  180723 one-eight-oh/zero-seven-two-three

- Say double and triple numbers like this:

769955	seven-six-**double nine-double five**	or
	seven-six-**nine nine-five five**	
122246	one-**double two two**-four-six	or
	one-**two double two**-four-six	or
	one-**two two two**-four-six	

Can/May I have your email address, please?

Saying email addresses

- Say words in email addresses as complete words but individual letters on their own.

  e. g. abgreen@quicknet.com a-b-green

- Say symbols like this:

@	at
.	dot
-	dash (or hyphen)
–	underscore
/	(forward) slash

- British firms' addresses normally end with.co.uk, said as 'dot co dot uk' ('co' rhymes with 'no'). American firms' addresses normally end with.com, said as 'dot com'.

e.g.	s_spence@browns.com	s underscore spence at browns dot com
	james-stewart@dsg.co.uk	james dash stewart at d s g dot co dot uk

Getting out of trouble

I'm sorry, I didn't get/understand that. Could you repeat it/say it again, please?

Could you speak more slowly/a little louder,please?

One moment, please. I'll put you through to somebody who can speak English (better than I can).

Saying goodbye

Thank you (very much) for your call. Goodbye.

Goodbye and thanks a lot/thank you (very much) for your help.

2 Arranging appointments

Asking for an appointment

I'd like to make an appointment to see..., please.

Would it be possible for me to see..., please?

Fixing a time and date

Do you have any particular date in mind?

How/What about (10 o'clock) on/next/ this coming (Wednesday)/on (the 15th)?

Would (10 o'clock) on/next/this coming (Wednesday) on (the 15th) be all right/convenient?

Saying dates

written	spoken	
6 June 2005 6th June 2005	the sixth of June, two thousand and five	(usual in British English)
June 6, 2005 June 6th, 2005	June (the) sixth, two thousand-five	(usual in American English)

Accepting and rejecting suggestions

No problem. (12.30) on/next / this coming (Tuesday)/on (the 23rd) will suit me fine/very well.

Yes, I can make it by (12.30) on/next (Tuesday)/on (the 23rd).

I'm afraid... has a meeting/another appointment then.

Unfortunately,... is not here/on a business trip/on holiday then.

Closing

Fine. I'll/We'll look forward to seeing you on (Wednesday the 22nd), then.

We'll expect you at (4pm) on (Wednesday the 22nd).

C Practising language

1 Use the English alphabet to dictate these abbreviations to your partner. Swap roles at least once. Then match each group of abbreviations with a cateeory from the box.

1 AA[1]-BA [2]-KLM[3]-SAS[4]-TWA[5]
2 ABC[1]-ARID[2]-BBC[3]-CNN[4]-RTL[5]
3 BASF[1]-BMW[2]-GMC[3]-IBM[4]-MAN[5]-VAG[6]
4 ISO[1]-NAFTA[2]-UN[3]-WTO[4]-WWF[5]

airlines
broadcasters
international organisations
manufacturers

2 First, read the model dialogue below to see how to spell out names. Then use the English alphabet and the international spelling code *(see page 16)* to role-play the dialogue with a partner using names from the box. Swap roles at least once.

You Can you tell me your last name, please?
Partner Of course. It's Hughes.
You Could you spell that for me, please?
Partner Sure. It's H-U-G-H-E-S.
You Sorry, is that 'S' for Sierra?
Partner That's right.
You Thanks, Ms Hughes.

Mr Hidvegi	Mr Ogunyemi
Ms Kepuska	Ms Piatkowski
Mr Laroussi	Mr Rozendaal
Mr Müller (ue)	Ms Steinmaier

3 Read the sentences to your partner, who should note down the phone numbers. Swap roles at least once.

1 My number's 0044 for the UK, then 141 for Glasgow, then 678 8430.
2 You can reach me on my mobile. The number's 0164, then 6453682.
3 The number of my hotel is 0221 for Cologne, then 723132.
4 We've moved. Our new number is 07531 for Constance, then 189707.
5 Can you fax confirmation, please? The number's 0031 for the Netherlands, then 182 for Gouda, then 330061.
6 You can phone Rolf direct on 030 for Berlin, then 8978584-09.

4 Dictate the email and website addresses to your partner. Swap roles at least once.

1 info@ifabs.co.uk
2 oduval@wanadoo.fr
3 anton.riedesel@aon.at
4 www.bbc.co.uk/radio4
5 www.save-whales.org
6 www.hrs.com

5 Dictate the dates to your partner. Only give the year when necessary. Swap roles once.

EXAMPLE: the date of the reunification of Germany
the third of october, nineteen-ninety

1 today's date
2 your date of birth
3 the date you last went to the cinema
4 the date of your last English test
5 the date of the next public holiday
6 a date that you will never forget

Listening comprehension

4 **6 Listen to the dialogue. Which of the following expressions do you hear? Each time only one of the two items is correct.**

1 a How may I help you?
  b Can I help you?

2 a Can you put me through to... ?
  b May I speak to...?

3 a May I ask who's speaking, please?
  b Who's calling, please?

4 a Hold the line, please.
  b I'll just put you through.

5 a May I speak to... ?
  b Is... there, please?

6 a I'm afraid... is busy at the moment.
  b I'm afraid... is in a meeting at the moment.

7 a I'll call again later.
  b I'll ring again tomorrow.

8 a Would you like to leave a message?
  b Can I take a message?

Now put the other expressions from above into the following dialogue. Two of the items do not fit at all.

Geoff Good afternoon. Smith and Co....[1] ?
Julia Good afternoon. Can I speak to Mr Smith, please?
Geoff ...[2] ?
Julia It's Julia Gordon from Kramer Ltd.
Geoff ...[3] , Ms Gordon.
Sarah Good afternoon. Mr Smith's office. Sarah Jones speaking.
Julia Hello. This is Julia Gordon from Kramer Ltd. Is Mr Smith there, please?
Sarah ...[4] . But he should be free at about 3 o'clock. ...[5] ?
Julia Could you tell him I called and...[6] , please?
Sarah Of course. Bye.
Julia Goodbye.

3 Office communication: emails

Model emails: making and confirming appointments, making and confirming hotel reservations, invitations and thank-you letters

Useful phrases: making appointments; making hotel reservations; invitations and thank-you letters

When to write emails

Most business correspondence deals with routine business matters, such as buying and selling. However, correspondence dealing with things like appointments, travel arrangements or hotel accommodation also needs to be sent, generally as emails. Unlike business letters, emails make use of spoken language, i.e. **short forms** (*it's, hasn't, we'd*) and an informal style, e.g. *Please let us know...* rather than *We would be grateful if you could advise us...* In fact, if you want to use a more formal style, then it is better so send a letter.

How to write emails

Salutation	Good morning/afternoon, (Name) Dear(Name) *Hello/Hi* (Name)	standard quite formal informal, particularly *Hi*
Subject	Say clearly what the email is about, for example, *I'm just writing about...* If you are answering an email, say something like *Thank you/Thanks for your email about...*	
Close	Thank the other person for his or her trouble/help,or say that you hope the arrangements you have made are satisfactory. Always ask the other person to get in touch if necessary.	
Signing off	*Yours sincerely/faithfully* sounds too formal in emails.Write something like *Best regards/ wishes, All the best* or simply *Yours.*	

The situation

Kent Casings Limited is a British manufacturer of clear plastic cases for CDs, DVDs and video games. It is situated in Ashford in Kent, not far from the tunnel terminal at Cheriton.

Plastex GmbH in Zwickau is a German manufacturer of advanced plastics. It supplies Kent Casings with plastics for many of its products.

Kate Medway is head of purchasing at Kent Casings. She often deals with Plastex. *Joe Davis* is Kate's personal assistant or 'PA'.

Rolf Schubert is the export manager at Plastex. Kent Casings is one of his biggest customers, so he and his secretary, *Julia Graf*, have a lot of contact with Kate and Joe.

A Model emails

1 Making and confirming appointments

Julia Graf and Joe Davis are arranging for Julia's boss, Rolf Schubert, to visit Kate Medway in Ashford.

From:	Julia Graf<julia.graf@plastex-zwickau.de>
To:	<joe.davis@kencas.co.uk>
Cc:	keine
Sent:	Wednesday, 8. May 20.. 14:56
Subject:	Mr Schubert's trip to UK

Good afternoon Joe

Mr Schubert asked me to get in touch with you about his visit to you next month.

Mr Schubert will be travelling to the UK by car through the Channel Tunnel on Sunday 6 June, so his first full day in England will be Monday 7 June.

As you're only about 20 km from the tunnel, would it be possible for Mr Schubert to visit you on either Monday 7 June or Friday 11 June?

Could you also let me know what Ms Medway would like to discuss at the meeting?

Thanks a lot for your trouble, Joe, and please get in touch if you have any queries.

Best wishes

Julia

From: Joe Davis <joe.davis@kencas.co.uk>
To: <julia.graf@plastex-zwickau.de>
Cc: Kate Medway <kate.medway@kencas.co.uk>
Sent: Friday, 10 May 20.. 11:18
Subject: Mr Schubert's trip

Good morning Julia

Thanks for your mail about Mr Schubert's plans.

I've now spoken to Kate and she says that Friday 11 June would be best because she's tied up all morning on the seventh.

As Kate thinks they'll need at least four and a half hours together, it would be best if Mr Schubert could arrive here at about 10 am. They could perhaps go to lunch at the Old Mill from 12.30 to about 2.

As far as the agenda goes, Kate would particularly like to discuss the delivery schedule for next year, your new scratch-and impact-resistant plastic and some problems with the IPC plastic for CD cases.

Well, that's about it, Julia. Could you please let me know your thoughts as soon as possible? Thanks a lot. Please get in touch if you have any questions.

Best wishes, also to Mr Schubert

Joe

a **Answer the questions about the first email.**

1 Who is the email from, and who is it to? When was the email sent?
2 How is Mr Schubert travelling to England?
3 Why does Mr Schubert want to visit Ashford on either his first or last day in England?
4 Apart from fixing a date, what other information does the sender ask for?

b **Say if the statements about the second email are true (T), false(F) or you can't say because the information is not given in the email(–). Correct the false sentences.**

1 Kate is in a planning meeting all morning on Monday.
2 Kate thinks she'll need about four and a half hours with Mr Schubert.
3 Kate says Mr Schubert can come at anytime he wants on 11 June.
4 Kate and Mr Schubert will have lunch in the staff canteen.
5 Joe is joining Kate and Mr Schubert for lunch at the Old Mill.
6 Kate wants to talk about breakage problems with IPC plastic.

From: Julia Graf<julia.graf@plastex-zwickau.de>
To: <joe.davis@kencas.co.uk>
Cc: keine
Sent: Friday, 10. May 20.. 14:56
Subject: Re: Mr Schubert's trip

Hi Joe

Thanks for your email about Mr Schubert's visit to Ashford.

Friday 11 June is fine, but Mr Schubert would like to start at 10.30 instead of 10, finishing at around 4, of course. This is because he's spending the night in Oxford and driving down to Ashford after an early breakfast on Friday. I hope this change is okay with Ms Medway.

And now to the agenda. As well as Ms Medways's three points, Mr Schubert wants to explain our new discounts for volume orders. However, as the new system increases Kent Casings' discount, this will probably only take ten minutes or so!

Well, I think that's all for now. Please mail me if there are any problems.

All the best

Julia

c Complete the sentences with details from the email.

1 Mr Schubert would like to start at...[1] am instead of...[2] am because he is driving to...[3] from...[4].
2 ...[1] would also like to talk about Plastex's new discounts for...[2] orders.
3 ...[1] does not think Mr Schubert will need more than about...[2] minutes because the new...[3] increases Kent Casings'...[4].

2 Making and confirming hotel reservations

Kate Medway has offered to find Mr Schubert a hotel for his visit and has asked Joe to book a room. The email is to The Garden House in Marsham confirming a telephone reservation.

From:	Joe Davis <joe.davis@kencas.co.uk>
To:	<reception@garden-marsham.co.uk>
Cc:	none
Sent:	Tuesday, 14 May 20.. 10:43
Subject:	Confirmation of reservation

Good morning

Further to our telephone conversation earlier this morning, I would like to confirm my reservation of a single room with ensuite bathroom for Mr Rolf Schubert for one night from Friday 11 June 20.. to Saturday 12 June, including full breakfast.

Mr Schubert will be arriving during the early evening and will require off-road parking.

As agreed, please send the invoice to me at Kent Casings Ltd, 22-26 London Road, Ashford, TN8 2BN.

Thank you for your trouble, and please get in touch if you have any questions.

Regards

Joe Davis

Join sentence parts 1-8 with a-j to make true statements. Two items in list a-j do not fit at all.

1 Before closing, Joe told the hotel
2 He agreed with the hotel that the invoice
3 Joe asked for a full breakfast
4 Joe Davis sent an email to
5 Joe had telephoned the hotel reception
6 Joe told the hotel that the guest
7 The purpose of the email was
8 The reservation was for a single

a earlier on the same morning.
b Julia in answer to her query about parking.
c room for one night for Rolf Schubert.
d The Garden House on 14 May.
e to be included in the price of the room.
f to confirm a telephone reservation.
g to contact him if there were any queries.
h to let him know about conference facilities.
i would also require off-road parking.
j would be sent to him at Kent Casings.

3 Invitations and thank-you letters

In this email, Rolf Schubert invites Kate Medway to have dinner with him on his last evening in England.

From:	Rolf Schubert<rolf.schubert@plastex-zwickau.de>
To:	<kate.medway@kencas.co.uk>
Cc:	keine
Sent:	Monday, 20. May 20.. 15:11
Subject:	Invitation

Dear Kate

Julia Graf has told me about the arrangements for my visit to Ashford on 11 June, which I'm already looking forward to. Thank you particularly for finding me a room for Friday night at your expense. That's very generous of you.

Joe Davis says that the hotel has a good restaurant, and I am now wondering whether you would like to join me for dinner there on Friday evening. I'm sure that I'd enjoy your company at the end of a hard week!

Perhaps you'd let me know whether you can accept this invitation so that we can reserve a table.

With best regards

Rolf

In this email, Kate accepts Rolf's dinner invitation.

Good afternoon, Rolf

Many thanks for your kind invitation to have dinner with you at The Garden House on Friday 11 June, which I'm delighted to accept. I'm already looking forward to it!

I hope you'll let me return your generosity when I visit you in Zwickau in the autumn.

All the best

Kate

B Useful phrases

1 Making appointments

Mr/Ms... would like to make an appointment to visit Mr/Ms...

If possible,... would like to visit you on (23 June) at (5.30pm).

Should this time be inconvenient, please suggest another date.

As Mr/Ms... is in... on (19 April)/from (17) to (21 April), ...

...he/she would like to take the opportunity of visiting...

He/She would like to discuss future business opportunities with...

... explain our new/revised discounts/prices.

...deliver/present our latest catalogue to Mr/Ms...

... demonstrate/present our new product (line).

... introduce our new representative for... to Mrs/Ms...

2 Making hotel reservations

Do you have any single/double rooms (free) for the (4) nights from (3) to (7 November)?

We need/require... rooms for the... nights from... to...

I/We would like... single and... double rooms with ensuite facilities.

The double rooms should have double/twin beds.

I'd/We'd like to reserve... rooms for the... nights from... to...

The day of arrival is... and departure will be after breakfast on...

The room(s) should be as quiet as possible.

We would like/require spaces in the hotel garage/car park for(4) cars/vehicles.

I/We will also require a conference room/conference rooms for (25) participants/ people.

The conference room should be equipped with a video projector/an overhead projector/a flipchart/internet connection/...

Please confirm this reservation by email/fax.

Please send the invoice to... for the attention of...

...will meet all costs except for those for the bar/minibar/phone calls/pay-TV.

3 Invitations and thank-you letters

I/We would like to invite you to a reception/the opening of our new branch/dinner at/in... on...

I/We have (great) pleasure in inviting you to... at... on...

The celebrations/reception begin(s) at... and will last about... hours.

We would be delighted to welcome you to... on... and (very much) hope that you will be able to accept this invitation.

Thank you very much (indeed) for your kind invitation to... on..., which I/we are delighted to/would like to accept.

...am/are unfortunately unable to accept because of a business trip/a prior engagement.

Many thanks for a (very) pleasant day/ afternoon/evening, which I/we enjoyed very much.

C Practising language

1 Complete the email about a change to a room reservation with words or expressions from the box. Be careful. Two of the items do not fit at all.

are | arrive | be taken | change | going | Good morning
in touch | made | questions | regards | reservation | tomorrow | train
until 10:50 | won't arrive | your trouble

...[1]

I'm afraid that we have got to ...[2] the reservation we...[3] for Ms Sigrid Janssen because she isn't ...[4] to the Bristol Marine Fair after all. Her place will now ...[5] by Mr Klaus Beck.

All the other details of the ...[6] stay as they ...[7].

Just one last thing. Mr Beck...[8] at the hotel until about 11:30 pm as his ...[9] from London doesn't get to Bristol ...[10].

Thanks a lot for ...[11], and please get ...[12] if you have any ...[13].

Best ...[14]

2 Take turns at reading the sentences out to a partner using the short form of the expressions in *italics*.

EXAMPLE: *I will* send out the invoice tomorrow.
I'll send out the invoice tomorrow.

1 The *letter is* in the post.
2 My *name is*[1] Satly Winters.*I am*[2] Mr Cobb's secretary.
3 *She has* been working here for ages.
4 The goods *were not* properly packed.
5 *They will*[1] visit us when *they are*[2] in London.
6 I *do not*[1] think that *you will*[2] get the job.
7 *We would*[1] do much better if we *did not*[2] have to pay so much tax.
8 I *have not*[1] seen Jane all week.She *is not*[2] ill,is she?
9 You *must not* talk to customers like that.
10 I *have*[1] heard that Tony *will not*[2] be at the meeting.

3 **Choose which of the two words or expressions in *italics* would be more suitable for an email. Don't forget that in emails we use informal spoken language.**

You asked me to *let you know/~~inform you~~*[1] when our marketing manager, Mr Peter Baxter, *envisages visiting/plans to visit*[2] Canada with a view to *arranging/fixing*[3] a meeting.

Mr Baxter's *itinerary is/travel plans are*[4] now *essentially/more or less*[5] finalised, and he'll be in Montreal for two full days, arriving on 11 March and *departing/leaving*[6] again for Detroit, where he is *attending/going to*[7] the spring automotive fair, early on 14 March. He *flies back/returns by air*[8] to the UK on the seventeenth.

As/Due to the fact that[9] Mr Baxter would very much like to meet Mr O'Neill, he is *considering/wondering*[10] whether either the morning of 13 or 14 March would be *convenient/okay*[11]. The meeting *could/might*[12] take place either at Mr Baxter's hotel, the Monarch, or at Mr O'Neill's office, of course.

Could you please let me know which of the two dates would be *best/most suitable*[13] and where the meeting could take place? As *things are/this matter is*[14] now *becoming/getting*[15] rather urgent, I'd be glad of *an early/a prompt*[16] reply.

Thank you very much/ Very many thanks[17] for your *efforts/trouble*[18], and I look forward to hearing from you. Please *don't hesitate to contact us/let us know*[19] if you have any *queries/questions*[20].

4 **This email confirming a room reservation is complete, but the parts are mixed up. Arrange the email in the proper order.**

a I also wish to book a space in the hotel garage. Ms Klein's car is a VW Passat, registration number EN-UU107.

b Good afternoon

c I'd like to reserve a single room with ensuite facilities for two nights, as follows:

d Best regards

e Please note that Ms Klein won't arrive at the hotel before about 10.30 pm on 6 June.

f Guest Ms Birgit Klein
Arrival 06 June 20..
Departure 08 June 20..

g This is to confirm the phone reservation I made this morning.

h Thank you for your trouble,and please get in touch with me if you have any questions.

5 Study the bar chart and complete the sentences with details from the chart.

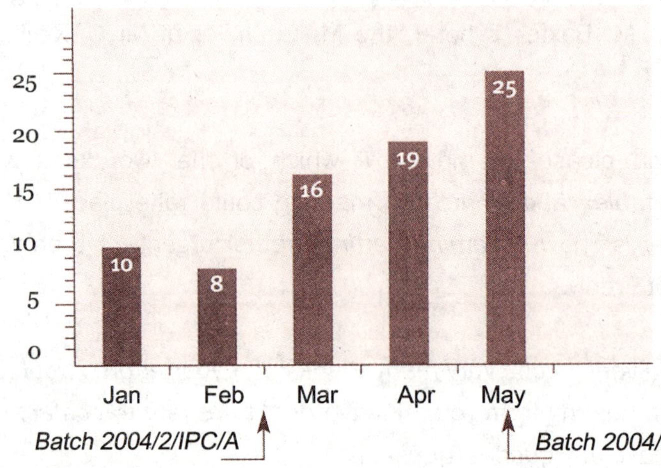

Bar chart showing Number of complaints about broken hinges on CD cases made of Plastex's IPC plastic at a production volume of 80,000 cases/month.

1 The complaints are about... on CD cases made of...
2 Kent Casings started using Batch 2004/2/IPC/A at the beginning of...
3 In January, there were... complaints, the normal number with a production volume of... cases per...
4 There's an... in complaints of over 200% between February and...
5 There are... complaints in April. That's almost... the amount there were in January.
6 Batch 2004/ .../IPC/... started to be used in the... of May.

Listening comprehension

5 6 **Listen to Joe's phone conversation with Kim Cameron of Star Car Hire and complete his notes. Then write an email to Kate with the details.**

Name (Company/Person): *Star Carf Hire/Kim Cameron*

Pick up date/place: ______

Return date/place: ______

Type of car: ______

Price: ______

Extra details: *Petrol...*

______

4 Enquiries

Model phone call, fax and letter: a general enquiry, a specific enquiry

Useful phrases: opening; background; request; close

What is an enquiry?

- There are two main kinds of enquiry: **general enquiries** and **specific enquiries.**
- The first asks for **general information** about a company's products, often in the form of a request for current catalogues, price-lists etc.
- A **specific enquiry** asks for an offer (for goods) or a quotation (for services). It gives exact details of the product or service required, including such information as order/model number and quantity. It may also give details of the customer's delivery requirements.

How to write enquiries

Enquiries have three or four parts, as follows:

Opening	If you are writing to a company for the first time, say where you got the firm's name and address from (see box) and who you are. If you are writing to a company you already do business with, start with giving a reason for the enquiry (see below).
Reason	Always say why you are making the enquiry. It can also be quite useful to give brief background information here.
Request	Say what you want the addressee to do. Make sure that you include all the necessary details. If you have any questions about discounts or delivery, for example, ask them here.
Close	Make a polite and friendly closing comment that motivates the addressee to answer your enquiry promptly.

Where buyers find suppliers

advertisement	We were interested to see your advertisement in *Export Focus.*
buyers' guide	We saw your entry in the *Universal Buyers' Guide.*
internet	Searching the internet,we were directed to your website.
recommendation	You were recommended to us by a customer, Carr & Sons of York.
trade fair	We visited your stand at the Medica trade fair in Düsseldorf.
trade organisation	The Chamber of Commerce in Leeds gave us your name.

A Model phone call, fax and letter

6 **1 Model phone call: a general enquiry**

Style Four Limited in London is looking for a supplier of stretch denim for its new range of S4F designer jeans. In this dialogue, Style Four's buyer, lane Adams, is telephoning Textil Dorn GmbH in Düsseldorf.

a **Listen to the dialogue and fill in the missing information.**

1 The caller's name is Jane...
2 The phone call is answered by...
3 Jane wants to speak to somebody in...
4 Pia puts Jane through to Mr...
5 Jane asks if Textil Dorn can supply...[1] cloth for...[2]
6 Specifically, Jane is interested in...[1] denim indifferent...[2]
7 Jane wants to see...[1] of...[2] denim.
8 Mr Dorn offers to send Jane his... of samples.

b **Answer the questions with *Yes/No*+short answer.**

EXAMPLE: Does Textil Dorn have an export department?
No, it doesn't.

1 Does Mr Dorn speak good English?
2 Does Jane speak German?
3 Is Textil Dorn a manufacturers' agent?
4 Does Jane ask about denim for jeans?
5 Is the denim for the new winter collection?
6 Can Textil Dorn offer an excellent range of Italian denim?
7 Does Jane want to see samples in two colours?
8 Will Jane fax the details?

c **Ask about the underlined parts.**

EXAMPLE: We can supply samples in six colours.
What can you supply?

1 Yes, I speak English.
2 I'd like to speak to someone from export.
3 I work for Style 4 in London.
4 Style 4 are looking for denim cloth for Jeans.
5 We are manufacturing a new range of jeans at the moment.
6 We want some light stretch denim for our summer collection.
7 Textil Dorn can supply black, white and dark blue denim material.
8 Mr Dorn is faxing the details because it is quicker than sending them by post.

2 Model fax: a general enquiry

Style 4 Limited

62 Albert Street
London E1 5RT

Tel	+44-(0)20-17 93 77
Fax	+44-(0)20-17 93 88
Email	info@styfo.co.uk
Internet	www.styfo.co.uk

Facsimile *message*

To:	Textil Dorn GmbH	**Date:**	22 November 20..
Fax no:	+40-211-783412	**Re:**	enquiry
For:	Mr Jens Dorn	**Pages:**	1

Dear Mr Dorn

Enquiry about denim

Further to our telephone conversation today, we would be obliged if you could send us samples of the high-quality light stretch denim for our new range of designer jeans that we discussed.

Could you please also forward us three copies each of your current catalogue and price-lists as well as details of your discounts for volume orders?

Thank you very much for your trouble, and as soon as we have examined and evalauted the samples for our purposes we will get in touch with you further.

Yours sincerely

Jane Adams

Jane Adams
Purchasing

If you have not received the number of pages shown above,
please contact us on +44-(0)20-17249377 at once.

Answer the questions with *Yes/No*+short answer as in 1b above.

1 Are Style 4's offices in Bristol?
2 Does Jane ask for an image brochure?
3 Have Jane and Mr Dorn done business before?
4 Does Jane work in the export department?

3 Modet Letter: a specific enquiry

Style 4 Limited

62 Albert Street
London E1 5RT

Tel +44-(0)20-17 93 77
Fax +44-(0)20-17 93 88
Email info@styfo.co.uk
Internet www.styfo.co.uk

Textil Dorn GmbH
Karlstraße 10

40593 Düsseldorf
Germany

10 December 20..

Dear Mr Dorn

Enquiry about denim

Thank you for reacting to our request for cloth samples so promptly, and having examined them, we are pleased to advise you that they appear to fulfil our requirements in every way.

We would therefore be grateful if you could submit a firm offer according to the following details:

1 eight (8) rolls, light stretch denim, blue, LSD 873B
2 four (4) rolls, medium stretch denim, black, MSD 728BK
3 as 2 above, white, MSD 728W

Please note that all prices quoted should include transport and delivery to our London premises.

Thank you for your trouble, and we look forward to receiving a competitive offer.

Yours sincerely

Style Four Limited

Jane Adams

Link the words 1-8 with the definitions a-h.

1 agent	**a** example
2 buyer	**b** (to) look at carefully
3 current	**c** large number
4 discount	**d** lower price fortrade buyers
5 (to) examine	**e** offer to supply a service on certain terms
6 quotation	**f** firm or person that acts for another firm or person
7 sample	**g** purchaser
8 volume	**h** up-to-date

B Useful phrases

1 Opening

We see from your entry in... that...

We note from your advertisement in ... of... that...

When we visited your stand at the... trade fair, we were interested to see that...

We understand from your sales brochure/leaflet that...

You have been recommended to us by a mutual customer, who informed us that...

... you manufacture/produce... for the leisure/steel/... industry.

... your company supplies... at competitive prices.

... you offer a wide range of...

2 Background

We are a leading importer/manufacturer/wholesaler of...

At present, we are extending our range of...

At the moment, we are planning to launch a new...

We are launching a new range of... next year/shortly/...

There is a growing market in... for... at a competitive price.

We are (therefore) interested in...

For this reason, we are in the market for...

3 Request

Please send us your new/latest catalogue and current price-list.

Please quote your prices net/gross.

Please send us... samples/specimens of your... for our inspection.

Would you please arrange for your representative to visit us?

We would (also) appreciate details of delivery periods.

Could you (also) please send us information on trade/volume discounts?

We would also appreciate information about your terms of payment.

Should you have any questions/queries, please get in touch with me/us.

4 Close

Thank you in advance for your assistance/help.

We look forward to hearing from you shortly/soon.

We would be grateful for an early reply.

We hope to hear from you again in due course.

C Practising language

1 **Complete the letter with words and expressions from the box. Be careful. Three words or expressions do not fit at all.**

address | brochure | buyers | clothing | company | edition | enclosing
faithfully | fashion | grateful | information | interested | manufacture
~~Request~~ | retail outlets | sale | samples | sincerely | suppliers
testing purposes | trade discounts | trouble | zip-fasteners

Dear Sir or Madam

Request[1] **for samples**

We are a medium-sized German...[2] which specializes in the...[3] of high-quality men's...[4] for sale through our own...[5]. We obtained your name and...[6] from the current...[7] of *Fashion Trades Buyers' Guide* as...[8] of buttons, press-studs,...[9] and other accessories for upmarket ...[10] products.

We would be...[11] if you could send us...[12] of your products for...[13]. We would also be...[14] to hear about your...[15] for volume orders.

Thank you for your...[16] and we look forward to hearing from you soon.

For your own ...[17], we have pleasure in...[18] a copy of our company image...[19].

Yours...[20]

(...)

2 Choose the word that fits best.

Dear Ms Adams

We are *delifghted* /~~*grateful*~~[1] to send you our standard *offer/selection*[2] of denim *examples/samples*[3] with this letter.

We also *enclose /insert*[4] three copies of our *actual/latest*[5] catalogue and *contemporary/current*[6] price-list. You will find details of our *discounts / rebates*[7], including those for *bulk /volume*[8] orders, on the back page of the price-list.

However, we are *eager/willing*[9] to discuss *special/unusual*[10] additional discounts for *periodic/regular*[11] orders.

If you have any *enquiries/queries*[12], please do not hesitate to *contact/get in touch with*[13] me.

Yours *faithfully/sincerely*[14]

(...)

3 Read the email and then match the underlined parts from the email to their more formal equivalents a-o.

I got[1] your email address off the web[2]. Anyhow, a mate[3] of mine was going through some old bike mags[4] the other day[5], and he saw[6] your ad[7] about BSA, Matchless and the rests[8].

We're dealers in old bikes like them[9] so we're always looking for original parts for them. For example, right now[10] I'm desperate for[11] a fuel tank for a 1938 Matchless 500. Any chance?[12]

Can you still supply this kind of stuff?[13] If yes,[14] please give us a ring.[15]

a advertisement

b at present

c back numbers of motorbike magazines

d call me

i from the internet

j I am urgently looking for

k If you are able to do so

l obtained

e Can you help me?
f classic bikes of this type
g discovered
h friend
m recently
n similar makes
o type of product

4 **Put the sentences of this enquiry into the correct order.**

a As a supplier of tennis equipment and clothing,we are currently expanding our range and wish to start supplying women' s wear as well as men' s wear.
b Dear Sir or Madam
c Purchasing Manager
d Thank you in advance for your help.
e We look forward to hearing from you soon.
f We saw your advertisement in the July issue of 'Fashion World' and were particularly interested by your range of sportswear.
g Yours faithfully
h We would also appreciate information about volume and trade discounts.
i Karen McDonald
j We would, therefore,be very grateful if you could send us a copy of your brochure, as well as an up-to-date price-list.

D Writing letters

Use the material in the box to complete the enquiry about exercise cycles for fitness studios.

Opening

- express interest in products, refer to an advertisement in 'Health and Fitness World' magazine

Background information, reason for enquiry

- you are a Munich-based fitness-centre chain
- you are particularly interested in exercise cycles 'ProMedic'

Request

- ask for a representative to call, as well as price-lists and terms of business
- also appreciate information about discounts

Close

- thank addressee for their trouble
- look forward to hearing from them

Dear Sir or Madam

We saw your advertisement in the latest issue of 'Health and Fitness World' magazine and...

5 Offers and quotations

Model letter: an offer

Useful phrases: opening; details; terms; close

What are offers and quotations?

Offers and quotations are both answers to a specific enquiry (see Unit 4). However, in normal usage, an **offer** relates to **goods**, and a **quotation** to **services.**

They tell the customer on what **conditions** (price, discount, delivery, terms of payment) the seller is willing to supply the goods or services required.

In the case of 'off-the-shelf' products of no great value, **standard offers**—i.e. offers without any special terms—are generally made by simply completing a form. You will usually find the supplier's **Terms and Conditions of Business** on the back of the form, often in small print. Read these carefully as they are legally part of the offer or quotation.

Offers or quotations that involve **special terms**, such as a higher discount or more generous terms of payment, can be in letter form (see below).

How to write offers or quotations

Opening	Refer to the original enquiry, with the date. You can also say what the enquiry was about.
Details	Give clear details of quantity,product,order number and price in tabular form. You can take these details from the enquiry. Depending on the product, they can also include things like colour and finish, of course.
Terms	Give clear, complete and correct information about trade discounts, volume/quantity discounts,possible cash discounts, terms of payment and means of delivery here.
Close	Thank the addressee for their enquiry and ask them to get in touch with you if they have any questions. You can also say that you would appreciate an order, but do not overdo it.

A Model letter

An offer

TextilDorn GmbH

karlstr.10.D-40593 Düsseldorf
Telephone: +49-(0)211-78 34 11
Telefax: +49-(0)211-78 34 12
Email: info@textildorn.de
Internet: www.texildorn.de

Style Four Limited
62 Albert Street
London El 5RT

18 December 20..

Dear Ms Adams

Offer for stretch denim

Thank you for your enquiry for denim of 10 December.

We are pleased to send you the following offer:

1	eight (8) rolls, light stretch denim, blue, LSD 873B	€7.50/m:	€600.00
2	four (4) rolls, medium stretch denim, black, MSD 728BK	€9.50/m:	€380.00
3	as 2 above, white, MSD 728W	€9.50/m:	€380.00

All prices include free delivery and transport to your London premises at 62 Albert Street, London El 5RT.

We confirm that these prices are 12.5% below list. We are willing to offer a further cash discount of 2.5% on the quoted price for payment in full within a fortnight of receipt of goods.

The consignment will be dispatched by road from Milan immediately upon receipt of order.

Thank you for your interest, and we would be delighted to receive your order. If you have any questions, please do not hesitate to get in touch with me.

Yours sincerely

Jens Dorn

Jens Dorn

B Useful words and phrases: offers and quotations

1 Opening

Thank you for/With reference to/Referring to your enquiry of...

We refer to your enquiry of...

With reference to your telephone call of...

2 Details

... we have pleasure in submitting the following offer/quotation:

We are pleased to send you our offer/quotation, as follows:...

3 Terms

We are pleased/willing to give/offer...

... a/an introductory/trade/volume discount of... % off list price.

... a cash discount of... % for payment/settlement within... days/a fortnight.

All prices are net.

The prices are EXW/FOB Cuxhaven/CIF Tilbury/...

Delivery will be made...

The consignment/goods/order will be dispatched...

... immediately on receipt of order by air/rail/road/sea.

... within 7/15/... days of receipt of order.

Payment should be made...

... in advance.

... on delivery (P/D).

... cash with order (CWO).

... on receipt of (the) consignment/goods/order.

... according to our usual terms and conditions of business.

... within 10/3o/... days of delivery.

... by irrevocable and confirmed letter of credit.

This offer/quotation is valid for... weeks/ months after the above date.

This offer/quotation is binding/firm until 30 June/...

This offer is subject to confirmation by 30 June/...

4 Close

Thank you (again) for your interest/enquiry.

We are sure/certain (that)...

We hope/trust (that)...

... you will be satisfied with our offer/products.

... you will take advantage of this offer/quotation.

If you have any questions/queries,...

Should you require any further information,...

... please contact/get in touch with me/ the undersigned/us.

We look forward to doing business with you.

C Practising language

1 Complete the letter with the missing words from the box. Note that there are three more words than you need.

business | cash discount | customers | depending | discounts | enquiry | excess | fortnight | further | grant | hesitate | interest | invoice | look forward | orders | pleased | receiving | ~~refer~~ | reminder | settlement | trade | volume | weeks

We *refer*...[1] to your...[2] of 23 April about our trade and volume...[3] .

We...[4] a standard...[5] discount of 10% on all...[6] from commercial...[7]. In addition, we offer...[8] discounts of between 3% and 6% on orders in...[9] of € 2000,...[10] on the size of the order.

We are also...[11] to allow a...[12] of 1.5% for...[13] within two...[14] of receipt of...[15].

Thank you for your...[16] , and please do not...[17] to contact me if you have any...[18] questions.

We...[19] to...[20] an order from you.

2 Choose the most suitable term.

Thank you for your *enquiry/query/question*[1] of 20 January. We are *glad/happy/pleased*[2] to submit the following *offer/quotation/tender*[3] for fitness machines: (...)

Please *note/realise/understand*[4] that all prices include *delivery/despatch/distribution*[5] to your Bremen *location/property/stores*[6] at Wiesenstraße 9 by road.

We *affirm/confirm/ensure*[7] that these prices are 15% below list as an introductory *favour/offer/ reward*[8]. We are willing to offer a *discount/rebate/reduction*[9] of 12.5% on *duplicate/repeat/return*[10] orders up to a *value/total/worth*[11] of € 5000 and 15% on orders above that *amount/total/volume*[12].

We are also *content/ready/willing*[13] to allow a cash discount of 2.5% on invoice price for *balance/paying/settlement*[14] within a fortnight of *getting/receiving/receipt*[15] of invoice.

The *goods/material/stuff*[16] will be dispatched *immediately/instantly/simultaneously*[17] on *delivery/presentation/receipt*[18] of order.

We hope that you are *content/gratified/satisfied*[19] with this offer, and we would be delighted to do *business/dealings / trade*[20] with you.

3 Complete the phrases with prepositions from the box.

about | for | in | on | to (3x) | under | with

1 (to) depend	... sth
2 (to) get	...[1] touch...[2] sb
3 (to) phone sb	... sth
4 (to) refer	... sth
5 (to) relate	... sth
6 (to) thank sb	... sth
7 (to)look forward	... doing sth
8 (to)put sb	... pressure

4 Form questions to ask about the underlined part of the statements.

EXAMPLE Barbara works in Brussels now.
Where does Barbara work now?

1 The goods were late because of bad weather in France.
2 I spoke to Janet Brown when I rang the firm.
3 Ajax Computers has placed an order for 500 CD burners.
4 You can place an order by completing an order form.
5 The enquiry was for CD burners.
6 The new delivery is in the stores.
7 I sent Hilary the offer by email.
8 Ben dealt with A jax's complaint.

Listening comprehension

7 **5 You are Pat King. (This name is used for both men and women.) You work in sales at Wessex Fitness Technology Ltd. Listen to the phone call and fill in the key details.**

Wessex Fitness Technology Ltd.

telephone message

Call taken by: .... Time/Date: *11:12, 4 Nov 20..*

Call from: ....

Caller: ....

Subject: .... *, Ref* ....

Product: .... *, Cat No* ....

Action agreed: *Copy of offer will be sent out* .... *,number* ....

Action by: *Self* ....

Initials: ....

D Writing letters

Use the material below to write an offer about camping equipment.

Think up a name and address for your German company and for the British supplier of such products. Add any relevant details such as quantities, models etc.

Opening

- Thank you for your enquiry about tents/... of (Datum).
- Thank you for your interest in our products.
- We refer to your enquiry about sleeping bags/... of (Datum).

Details

- We are happy to send/submit an offer for tents/sleeping bags/... as follows:

Terms

- All prices include delivery to...
- We are pleased/willing to give/offer a trade/volume/introductory discount of...%.
- The consignment/goods will be despatched by air/road within... days on receipt of order.

Close

- Thank you again for your interest in our products.
- We are certain/sure that you will be (entirely) satisfied with our products.
- Please do not hesitate to contact/get in touch with us if...
- We look forward to receiving an order/doing business with you in due course/ the future.

6 Orders and acknowledgements

Model letters: an order, an acknowledgement

Useful phrases: orders (opening, placing an order, delivery terms); acknowledging an order; cancellation of an order

What are orders and acknowledgements?

When the buyer places an order, he enters into a **contract of sale** with the seller for the delivery of goods and services. The offer (or catalogue plus price-list) and often the seller's **terms and conditions** are the basis for this contract. The order states the exact amounts and types of goods required. It is also common practice for the buyer to repeat the exact **terms of the offer** (discounts, terms of payment and delivery). Today the buyer often only needs to fill in and sign an order form.

The seller only needs to confirm the order, i.e. to write an **acknowledgement of order**, when the terms of the offer have been changed by the buyer.

It may also be necessary to write when the seller cannot supply the goods as offered (goods currently not available or out of stock, delays). In this case, the seller may consider offering a different, but similar, product (**new offer**) and the buyer is expected to agree to the new offer.

How to write orders and acknowledgements of orders

	Orders	Acknowledging the order
Opening	Refer to the offer and say that you wish to place an order.	Thank the customer for the order.
Details	Specify your order (quantity, product number, type, price, etc.)	Say when you expect to deliver.
Terms	Confirm the terms and conditions. (Specify a date for delivery)	
Close	Close with a polite phrase.	Close with a polite phrase.

A Model letters

1 An order

Style 4 Limited
62 Albert Street
London E1 5RT

Tel +44(0)20-17 93 77
Fax +44-(0)20-17 93 88
Email info@styfo.co.uk
Internet www.styfo.co.uk

Textil Dorn GmbH
Karlstraße 10
D-40593 Düsseldorf
Germany

22 December 20..

Order for denim material

Dear Mr Dorn

Thank you for your prompt reply to our enquiry. We would now like to place the following order:

1	10 rolls, light stretch denim, blue	LSD 873B	€ 7.50/m =€ 750.00
2	6 rolls, medium stretch denim, black	MSD 728BK	€ 9.50/m =€ 570.00
3	as 2 above, white	MSD 728W	€ 9.50/m =€ 570.00

Please note that we have revised the quantities.

We accept the prices and terms as stated in your offer of 18 December. In view of the forthcoming Christmas break, we would ask you to arrange for delivery to be made in the first full week in January.

Thank you for dealing with our enquiry so quickly and we look forward to receiving the goods in due course.

Yours sincerely

Jane Adams

Jane Adams
Buyer

Replace parts of the letter above with the following. The answers are not necessarily in the same order.

1 Because of the approaching public holiday
2 replying so quickly
3 for us to receive the goods
4 altered the size of the order
5 You wilt notice
6 We agree to the terms and conditions of the offer

2 An acknowledgement

Friesenstr.12 04177 Leipzig Tel.0341/44 53 41
Fax 0341/44 53 42 34 E-Mail info@tessaconstruct.de
Internet www.tessaconstruct.de

tessa CONSTRUCTION

Henderson Engineering Ltd
Unit 23
Ash Industrial Estate
Flex Meadow
Harlow
Essex CM19 5TJ
England

13 October 20..

Contract No.2756/8

Dear Mr Cox

Please find attached three fully signed copies of the contract for the delivery of warehousing systems which you requested in your fax of 3 October.

You will note that we have included the amendments agreed in our recent exchange of faxes (confirmed and authorised in your fax of 10 October). These changes mainly concern the revised prices and terms of payment.

Please sign next to the changes we have made and return one copy of the contract for our files.

Meanwhile,we are processing your order and it should be ready for dispatch as agreed.

We look forward to hearing from you by return.

Yours sincerely

Angela Palm

Angela Palm

Correct these statements if necessary.

1 The letter is in reply to a message received on 3 October.
2 The copies enclosed need to be signed.
3 The contract has already been negotiated.
4 The contract will be signed on 3 October.
5 No changes have been made.
6 The changes were agreed to in a fax of 10 October.
7 There are probably changes regarding prices and terms.
8 All the changes need to be approved in writing.
9 The recipient should keep one copy.
10 The buyer will be informed when the order is ready for dispatch.

B Useful phrases

1 Orders

Opening

Thank you for sending us/letting us have your offer.

Thank you for your offer of... /We have received your offer of...

We have carefully examined/tested your samples/specimens.

We are pleased with both the quality of your samples and your prices.

Placing an order

We refer to/With reference to your offer of... (and) (we) would like to place the following order:

Having looked at the samples/specimens you sent us, we wish to order the following (for immediate delivery).

Our order is based on your catalogue number...

Please find enclosed/We enclose our order, number 8765, for the following items: ...

Delivery terms

The goods ordered must be delivered immediately.

We must insist that the goods be supplied within ten days.

If you are unable to/If you cannot deliver within this period...

Delivery should be franco domicile.

We accept your terms of payment and delivery.

Please confirm the above order as soon as possible.

2 Acknowledging an order

We refer/Referring/With reference to your order (number 4848) of 5 May...

We received your order for... today./We confirm your order Of 12 July.

We agree to your proposal to increase the volume/quantity discount to 20 per cent.

You will understand that we must insist on our terms of payment for initial orders.

We are, of course, prepared to consider the payment terms again at a later date.

Item number 487 is not available/not in stock/out of stock at the moment.

We require approximately ten days to complete your order.

We shall deal with/process your order as soon as possible.

3 Cancellation of an order

We wish to cancel our order.

Please delete the following items...

We reserve the right to cancel the order/to refuse (to take/accept) delivery if...

Please cancel all items that cannot be delivered/supplied by the end of the month.

Useful abbreviations

B/E bill of exchange	B/L bill of lading
C/P carriage paid	C/F carriage forward
COD cash on delivery	CWO cash with order
D/A documents against acceptance	D/O delivery order
D/P documents against payment	L/C letter of credit
VAT value added tax	

C Practising language

1 **Combine the verbs in group A with the appropriate nouns in group B.**

A	B
grant	an order
reserve	delivery
agree	from stock
examine	the requirements
guarantee	the samples
meet	to the terms and conditions
supply	a discount
place	the right

2 **Use the most suitable term in the box to replace the expressions in *italics* in the sentences below. There are more terms than you need.**

a fortnight | dispatch | expect delivery to be made | if you do not | is due
kindly accept | receipt of invoice | order volume | volume | warranty
we feel that | we reserve the right to | please let us know

1 *In our opinion*, your prices are too high for this market.
2 *Unless you* improve your terms, we will not be able to accept your offer.
3 We are placing this order on condition that you grant us a *quantity* discount of 15 per cent.
4 We *expect to receive the goods* within a week.
5 It is understood that payment *should be made* within two weeks of *the invoice being received.*
6 We will cancel our order if the goods are not delivered within *two weeks.*

7 We understand that your goods are supplied with a six-month *guarantee.*
8 *Kindly inform us* when the goods are ready for *shipment.*

3 **Use the following to form meaningful sentences. Add commas where necessary.**

1 for your offer/of 2 March/reached us/Thank you/today/which
2 Having examined/meet our requirements/to state that/we are pleased/ your goods/your samples
3 for the market/However/in which/are too high/we operate/your prices
4 more favourable discounts/or grant us / to accept/we are unable/Unless you can lower/your offer/your prices
5 are delivered/at the latest/by 15 April/is placed/on condition that/Our order/ the goods
6 for your order/our immediate attention/We thank you/which/will have
7 and accept your request/for payment/of 22 February/We acknowledge/ within 30 days net/your order
8 and risk/at your cost/Please note that/substandard goods/will be returned

Listening Comprehension

8 4 **Write a summary in English of the telephone conversation you hear.**

Role Play

5 **Role-play the following telephone conversation with a partner.**

A	B
introduction, mentions meeting at the trade fair, hopes it was successful for **B**	introduction, asks what he/ she can do
glad to hear that, thanks for prompt reply to enquiry, likes the designs and workmanship of garden furniture displayed at the fair	on the whole pleased with the business done
prices are higher than those of the competitors	short positive reaction
wonders whether prices and terms can be improved	reacts with surprise and asks for a suggestion
replies that in view of the number of outlets (more than 30 garden centres in south and central Germany) the order volume is likely to be very high	thinks that in view of the quality and workmanship prices are fair, asks about possible order volume
replies that initial order could be in the range of € 25,000, further orders to be expected	asks **A** to be more specific
agrees to 5 per cent discount, hopes that more generous discounts will be possible in future	is prepared to grant an additional volume discount of 5 per cent, could be reviewed for follow-up orders
polite end of conversation	thanks for order and will confirm new terms in writing, hopes he will be pleased with the goods, polite end of conversation

D Writing letters

1 **Use the phrases in the box to write a letter.**

Opening

- Thank you for your...
- We confirm the receipt of your fax/letter of...
- We are pleased to note/to accept your improved volume discount and payment terms.
- Thank you for revising your terms.

Details

- As we expect the demand for sunshades to be higher than we originally thought,...
- We can now offer your sunshades at even more competitive prices.
- We are confident we will attract even more buyer interest with these lower prices.

Terms/Solution

- We have therefore decided to increase our order/the order volume as follows: ...
- Please find our revised order enclosed.
- Your revised terms have persuaded us to increase the order volume as listed in the enclosed order form.
- You will be pleased to learn that we have decided to increase the number of units per item.

Close

- Thank you again for adjusting your terms and we look forward to receiving the goods as agreed.
- Thank you again for improving your terms and...
- We would like to confirm that you can still supply the goods by the date originally agreed.
- Thank you again and we look forward to receiving the goods in due course.

2 **Write a reply to this fax message.**

Bushmill Engineering LTD

11–15 O'Leary Street
Limerick Ireland
Tel 061 43679–0
Fax 061 43679–234
www.Bushmillengineering.com.ie
Email info@bushmillengineering.com.ie

FAX MESSAGE

Date:	*15 February 20..*	
To:	*Winter Maschinenbau GmbH Pforzheim*	*Fax 07231/46 47 3811*
For:	*Herr Wortmann*	
Pages:	*1*	
About:	***Order confirmation***	

Dear Mr Wortmann

During your visit to us in January, we placed a major order with you for the supply of metal working machines. At the time you promised to send us the relevant documentation immediately after your return to Germany. Unfortunately, we are still awaiting your confirmation of this order. We need the machines as soon as possible and would like you to confirm our order. Could you also inform us whether you would prefer payment by L/C or cash against documents? We have attached a copy of our order for your reference. We hope to hear from you very soon.

Yours sincerely

Ken McDougal

Ken McDougal
(Production Manager)

7 Dealing with orders

Model letters: asking for the reasons of a delay in delivery, reply stating reasons for delay, transport arrangements

Useful phrases: dealing with orders; supplier's delivery periods; buyer's request for delivery; transport arrangements

What happens when an order has been placed?

Once the order has been received and accepted, the supplier will get the goods **ready for dispatch.**

When goods are supplied from stock, delivery can be made immediately. If, however, the goods are made to the customer's specifications (**customised goods**), production may take longer. If the seller fails to deliver the goods on time, the customer usually sends an enquiry about the delay. Delays are especially serious with goods shipped abroad because complex matters of transportation (packing, means of transport, sharing of costs and risks, time schedules) need to be clarified (cf. **INCO-Terms**).

How to deal with order processing issues

	Enquiry about a delay in delivery	Replying to an enquiry about a delay in delivery	Dispatch. Shipping arrangements
Opening	Refer to the order and promised delivery date.	Refer to the enquiry about the delivery date.	Refer to the order.
Details	Express your surprise at the delay.	Apologise for the delay and state reason(s).	State that the goods are ready for shipment.
Action	State why you need the goods urgently. Indicate consequences of further delay.	State what you are going to do to speed up the delivery.	Give all the relevant details about the delivery.
Close	Express hope for speedy delivery. Close with a polite phrase.	(Apologise again.) Ask for understanding. Close with a polite phrase.	Express hope that goods will arrive safely. Close with a polite phrase.

A Model letters

1 Asking for the reasons for a delay in delivery

Leith Weaving Ltd
12 Palmerston Road
Tel 0131-45672-1
Forth Industrial Park
Leith EH15 4TG
Fax 0131-45672-240
Email: Ann.Spears@leithweaving.co.uk
Internet: www.leithweaving.co.uk

Leith Weaving

Langley Engineering Solutions (LES) Ltd
Cambridge Science Park
Milton Road
Cambridge
CB4 OGW

20 August 20..

Order for tartan fabrics

Dear Ms Soames

We are surprised that our goods (order no. 1186/27) have not arrived yet. In your letter of 11 July, you promised shipment by the beginning of August and we advised our customers accordingly.

We quite understand that delays are sometimes unforeseen and unavoidable. However. it is usual to at least inform the customer and we are rather disappointed that we did not hear from you about any problems.

We look forward to your reply.

Yours sincerely

Ann Spears

Ann Spears
(Buyer)

2 Reply stating reasons for delay

24 August 20..

Your order No. 1186/27

Dear Ms Spears

We acknowledge the receipt of your letter of 20 August and must apologise for the delay in the execution of your order. The last delivery of the tartan materials from the factory was slightly off-shade but, as we were expecting new supplies within a matter of days, we thought we did not need to write to you. We are sorry that you have been inconvenienced but want to assure you that your order has had our usual, careful attention.

A new consignment has arrived today so we can now begin manufacturing your goods and expect to deliver your order within the next few days.

We apologise once again for the delay and hope it has not caused you any serious trouble.

Yours sincerely

Judy Soames
(Sales Officer)

a Correct these statements about the letters.

1. Order no. 1286/37 is for tartan fabrics.
2. The order was due to be delivered by 20 August.
3. The buyer didn't advise his customers of the delivery date.
4. Delays are always unavoidable.
5. The customer was informed of the delay.
6. New fabric arrived on 22 August.
7. Ms Spears signs the letter dated 24 August.
8. The tartan materials were of a different colour from that ordered.

b Complete these phrases with the appropriate verbs from the letters.

1. to... shipment
2. to... a customer
3. to... from somebody
4. to... the receipt of a letter
5. to... for a delay
6. to... manufacturing
7. to... an order
8. to... serious trouble

3 Transport arrangements

Stolte & Hagen

Stolte&Hagen GmbH Oderstr.64 01109 Dresden

Tel0351-34 12 1-0 Fax0351-34 12 1-211 E-Mail Info@stolte-hagen.de www.stolte-hagen.de

Hartleby & Baines Ltd
245 Oldham Road
Halifax
HX12 4PZ

England

24 April 20..

Your order for plastic seats

Dear Mr Darling

Thank you again for your order of 21 March for plastic seats. The order is nearly complete and we expect to make delivery early next week.

The goods have been carefully packed and palletised for easy handling as agreed. As requested, we have arranged for the transport to be carried out by Spedition Sundermann, a local haulier.

They will contact you about further details and also issue a separate invoice for their transport services.

Please find our invoice enclosed. As per our contract, we expect settlement within a fortnight of receipt of the goods. We hope the consignment reaches you in good condition and thank you again for your order.

Yours sincerely

U. Hinrichs

U. Hinrichs

Here are some statements about the letter above. Ask questions about the parts in *italics* using the question words in brackets.

1 The order is *for plastic seats.* (what?)
2 Delivery can be made *early next week.* (when?)
3 The goods are palletised *for easy handling.* (why?)
4 *Spedition Sundermann, a local haulier,* will be responsible for transport. (who?)

5 The hauliers *will contact* Hartleby & Baines Ltd. (what?)

6 They will issue *a separate invoice for transport services.*(what?)

7 The invoice for the goods is *enclosed.* (where?)

8 They expect settlement of the invoice *within a fortnight of receipt of the goods.* (when?)

B Useful phrases

1 Dealing with orders

We received your order for... today./Thank you for/We confirm your order of 12 July.

Item number 487 is not available/not in stock/is out of stock at the moment.

Therefore, we cannot guarantee delivery by 4 March.

We require approximately ten days to complete your order.

We cannot start manufacture until August.

2 Supplier's delivery periods

We confirm the delivery date you stipulated/ requested/asked for in your letter.

We can deliver the goods earlier than agreed/immediately/by 10 August at the latest.

Our earliest delivery time would be in one month's time.

We shall have the goods ready for shipment by the beginning of May.

The goods you ordered await collection/are ready for collection/are ready for dispatch/shipment.

The delay in delivery is due to...

It will not be possible to deliver the goods within the agreed period of 2 months.

We have started the manufacture of your goods.

Delivery will take place within 4 months.

3 Buyer's request for delivery

Please let us know when delivery will be made.

This order is urgent and we would appreciate it if you could arrange for immediate shipment/delivery.

The delay in delivery has caused us considerable problems.

The goods must be delivered by the end of next month.

Delivery must be made on time.

We cannot accept the goods if they are not delivered on time.

We have not yet received the goods.

The consignment you promised to deliver on 13 February has not arrived yet.

4 Transport arrangements

Your order does not state/say/mention how the goods should be transported.

The cases have been collected by the carriers.

We shall send all the goods in a single consignment.

The consignment consists of two cases, each weighing 50 kilos.

The goods were dispatched/sent to you today/on 9 June.

The ship should arrive in Felixstowe on 21 July.

by rail
by air; as/by air freight
by ship
by lorry/truck; by road
carriage/freight paid
carriage/freight forward
exclusive/inclusive of freight/carriage

C Practising language

1 **Complete this letter using the words in the box. There are more items than you need.**

apologise for | are pleased | At this stage | be fair to | deal with orders | delay in delivery | due to | everything we can | keep you informed | order for | process your order | unfortunately | we are sorry | you will realise

Dear Mr Williams

Thank you for your...[1] laminated security glass of 5 July which we...[2] to confirm. However,...[3] to have to inform you that,...[4] the breakdown of one of our machines, there will be a...[5] of at least a week. We are doing...[6] to have the machine repaired as soon as possible. But...[7] that parts have to be flown in and fitted. To...[8] all our customers, we have decided to...[9] on a strict rota basis. We will...[10] about the progress of the repair work here....[11] we would like to thank you for your understanding and...[12] the inconvenience caused.

Yours sincerely

2 **Saying you are sorry.**
Use verbs or verbal expressions from the table to fill the gaps. You may have to change the structure of the following verb as well. Sometimes more than one answer is possible.

formal	informal/spoken
to apologise for | to excuse to offer one's apologies (for)	to regret | to be sorry

EXAMPLE: I... for being more than half an hour late.
I'm sorry for being more than half an hour late.

1 We... not to be able to deliver the machine by the date agreed in our contract.
2 We... for this delay. But it was not our fault.
3 I... to give you the wrong information.
4 I misread the order number. Please... me.
5 I... not to have told you about this earlier.
6 We realise that this late delivery has made trading difficult for you and...
7 Please... the late arrival of this consignment, which is entirely due to reasons beyond our control.
8 We... to have caused you this inconvenience.

3 **Decide which is the correct term. If in doubt, consult your dictionary.**

1 We acknowledge the delivery date you *commanded/demanded/stipulated* in your order.
2 The goods can be supplied earlier than *agreed/set up/contracted.*
3 The earliest *consignment/delivery/supply* date is two weeks from the date of your order.
4 We promise to start production upon *receipt/reception/recipe* of your order.
5 Please let us have your *commands/instructions/orders* for shipment as soon as possible.
6 Our delivery dates must be strictly *adhered to/obeyed/watched.*
7 Our forwarding agent will *contact you/contract you/inform you* regarding the details of the transport arrangements.
8 We are pleased to confirm that, in accordance with your *shipping/supply/ship* instructions, we have handed over your consignment to our forwarding agent today.

Listening Comprehension

9 4 **Listen to the first telephone conversation about a delivery problem and answer questions 1-5. Then listen to the second conversation and answer questions 6-10.**

Mr Cunningham wants to discuss a delivery problem with Ms Kourgialis.

1 Which company does Mr Cunningham work for?

2 Where has Ms Kourgialis gone?
3 Will Ms Kourgialis be back later in the day?
4 What message did the secretary take?
5 Does Ms Kourgialis have Mr Cunningham's number?

Ms Kourgialis phones Mr Cunningham the next morning.

6 Why wasn't Ms Kourgialis in the office on the day before?
7 What was the promised delivery date?
8 When will the goods be delivered?
9 What is the problem Mr Cunningham talks about?
10 What is the solution Mr Cunningham suggests?

Now take the part of Mr Cunningham and write a short memo for your principal.

D Writing letters

1 **Use suitable sentences from the list below to inform your customer about a delay in delivery.**

Opening
- Thank you (very much) for your order of...
- We are pleased to acknowledge receipt of your letter of...
- We have received your letter of...

Details
- (You will be pleased to learn that) All the items are in stock/are ready for dispatch/ can be shipped except for...
- (However,) we are sorry to have to inform you...
- We are sorry to say that...
- Due to an unexpectedly high demand, the following items are (temporarily) out of stock.
- Unfortunately, we are unable to supply these goods at present/ at the moment.

Action
- We expect new supplies within a week/fortnight at the latest.
- As new supplies are expected within a few days/a fortnight, we would suggest that we hold your order until then.

- Of course, we could send/dispatch the available goods immediately and ship the remainder (free of charge) as soon as the new supplies have come in.

Close

- We hope to hear from you soon.
- Please let us know what you want us to do.
- We apologise once again for the inconvenience and look forward to receiving your instructions by return.
- Thank you for your understanding and we promise to dispatch your goods as soon as possible.

2 **Write a letter/fax informing a customer about a delay in delivery for this order.**

Derby Warehousing Ltd

12-14 Leicester Street
Derby DE5 9BN
Tel 01332-75764-1
Fax 01332-75764-500
www.derby-warehouse.co.uk

Melchers & SchmittGmbH & Co KG
Fabrikzeile
95028 Hof
Germany

Order for shelving system Orion

Dear Mr Schumacher

We refer to your offer of 25 March and our telephone conversation of 1 April. We would like to place an order for the equipment of our entire warehouse with the Orion shelving system on the basis of your offer and the subsequent changes in prices and discount. Please find the full details in our supply contract, two copies of which are enclosed.

We would like to confirm the main points of this contract. It is agreed that the price of £275,000 covers the delivery and assembly of the shelving system at our premises.

The amount is payable in three instalments: £75,000 within a week of your acceptance of our order, £100,000 upon delivery of the equipment at our premises and the remainder after the full and satisfactory completion of the assembly.

The shelving system will be delivered in the second week of May and you will start assembly work within 5 days of delivery at the very latest.The assembly is scheduled to take a full working week. Penalty clauses apply in case of a delay in the assembly work.

Please sign the contract and return one copy to us.

We look forward to hearing from you in the near future.

Yours sincerely

Peter Fisher

Peter Fisher

Managing Director

8 Payments and reminders

Model letters: letter requesting payment, first reminder, second and final reminder, reply to a first or second reminder

Useful phrases: sending an invoice / a statement and asking for payment; reminder; delayed payment terms; making and confirming payment

How is payment obtained?

The seller usually sends the invoice when the goods have been delivered. The invoice includes the details of the transaction, the time allowed for payment and also the cash discount. If there are problems with the invoice (accounting errors, wrong goods etc.), the buyer will point out any **discrepancies** and can expect the mistake to be put right.

If payment is not made on time, the seller sends a friendly **request for payment**, often a standard letter combined with the offer of new goods. The **first reminder (collection letter)** is normally accompanied by a copy of the invoice and states a final date for payment. The second reminder is friendly but insistent in tone and gives the buyer a final **deadline for payment.** All the relevant details are stated and the possibility of legal action is mentioned.

How to deal with order processing issues

	Request for payment	First/second reminder	Reply to reminders
Opening	Refer to the transaction.	Refer to the transaction and state disappointment at not having received payment.	Refer to the transaction and apologise for delay.
Details	State that payment may have been overlooked.	Repeat payment terms. Remind the customers of duty to pay for goods/services.	State why payment was withheld.

(Continued)

Action	Ask for payment to be made.	Ask for payment to be made immediately and state period/date.	State that you are paying now or ask for extension. (Apologise again.)
Close	Close with a polite phrase.	Express hope for speedy settlement. Close with a polite phrase.	Thank the supplier for understanding. Close with a polite phrase.

A Model letters

1 Letter requesting payment

20 June 20..

<u>our invoice No. 5421/05</u>

Dear Ms Dixon

We refer to our consignment of video tapes and the attached invoice No.5421/05. According to our records we have not yet had any payment from you. We are sure our invoice has been simply overlooked. Please ensure that your remittance is made without delay.

Thank you for your attention.

Yours sincerely

Sylvia Fuchs

Sylvia Fuchs

2 First reminder

20 July 20..

Our invoice No.5421/05

Dear Ms Dixon

This is to inform you that, according to our records, we have not yet received the amount of £2,004.50 due from our invoice No. 5421/05. The amount is now more than eight weeks overdue. We would like to remind you that payment was due within a fortnight from the date of invoice and we kindly ask you to clear your account without further delay. If you have transferred the outstanding sum in the meantime, please disregard this letter.

We would appreciate it if you could send payment as soon as possible.

We look forward to receiving your remittance by return.

Yours sincerely

Sylvia Fuchs

Sylvia Fuchs

3 Second and final reminder

20 August 20..

Our invoice No.5421/05

Dear Ms Dixon

We are disappointed that we have to write to you again about the settlement of our invoice No. 5421/05. You will realise that the amount of £2,004.50 is now twelve weeks overdue. We fail to understand why we have received neither payment nor an explanation for your delay in clearing your account. We enclose a copy of our invoice for your information and must ask you to give this matter your immediate attention. Unless we receive your transfer within the next ten days or a satisfactory explanation for your delay in payment, we will have no choice but to turn the matter over to our solicitor. It is up to you now to help us to avoid such a step.

We hope to receive your remittance by return.

Yours sincerely

Sylvia Fuchs

Svlvia Fuchs

a Complete these sentences.

1 Two weeks ago we sent you a... of video tapes.
2 Our records show that... No. 5421/05 is still outstanding.
3 Please let us have your... promptly.
4 Payment is now more than eight weeks...
5 The letter can be... if payment of the... amount has been made in the meantime.
6 Ms Fuchs would... it if the customer paid the outstanding amount as soon as...
7 Ms Fuchs is looking forward to the account being settled...
8 Ms Fuchs writes to the customer a third time to ask for the... of invoice No. 5421/05.
9 Ms Dixon is asked to give the matter her...
10 If payment is not made immediately, a... will be asked to deal with the matter.

b Let's establish the facts.

1 What kind of product did the customer buy?
2 Can you remember the invoice number?
3 What is the invoice amount?
4 Work out when the invoice was due for payment.
5 What were the terms of payment?
6 How much time has passed between the date of invoice and the first reminder?
7 How much time has passed when the final reminder is sent?
8 What is the deadline for payment when the final reminder arrives?

4 Reply to a first or second reminder

baumann webwise
Die IT-Profis

Intelligent PC Supplies Inc
5736 14th Street NE
St. Paul
Minnesota MN 55232
U.S.A.

31 August 20..

Your request for payment

Dear Mr Cunningham

We refer to our order No. 2048X7 and your invoice G 4758 of 21 May and apologise most sincerely for the delay in clearing our account. Your reminders did not go unnoticed and it is certainly not our practice to exceed our credit periods.

It is due to events beyond our control that we delayed settling your account. Unfortunately, two of our best customers have recently gone out of business which made it difficult for us to meet all our financial obligations promptly, especially considering the current problematic business climate.

We are pleased to state, however, that our efforts to stabilise our cash flow are now beginning to pay off. Therefore, we have paid $10,000.00 today and will transfer the remainder of $10,345.00 in a month ' s time. We hope you will understand our situation and appreciate that we are making every effort to clear our account as soon as we can.

Thank you in advance for your understanding and patience.

Sincerely yours

Annika Tauber

Annika Tauber
(Accounts Dept)

baumann webwise GmbH
Naumburger Str. 27
04229 Leipzig
Tel 0341-879571-1
Fax 0341-87957-223
E-Mail info@webwise-leipzig.de
www. webwise-leipzig.de

Decide which parts of the letter above can be replaced by the following expressions. They are in the same order.

a Referring to
b we offer our sincere apologies
c in settling your invoice
d requests for payment
e we do not normally
f payment
g bankrupt
h commitments
i difficult business situation
j our attempts
k outstanding amount
l are doing all we can
m as quickly
n Yours truly

B Useful phrases

1 Sending an invoice/a statement and asking for payment

Please find enclosed/We enclose our invoice no. ... for the goods delivered to you on 3 May.

We kindly ask for early settlement of/ask you to settle our invoice by return.

We request payment of our invoice to account number...

We enclose our statement for the second quarter.

The total amount payable is...

We have already deducted the customary discount of... % from your invoice.

2 Reminder

Our invoice no.... is still unpaid.

As the unpaid/outstanding amount is considerably/four weeks overdue,...

Your account still shows a debit balance of...

Please let us have the amount due within the next few days.

We await your payment/remittance/transfer by... at the latest.

We wish to remind you that our terms of payment are...

We have as yet had no reply to our request for payment.

Despite our repeated requests for payment...

We must remind you that we only allow two weeks credit for first orders.

This is our last/final request for payment.

We must now insist on immediate payment/settlement of our invoice.

If we do not receive payment by the beginning of next month, we see no alternative but to take legal steps/action.

We have placed the matter in the hands of our lawyers/solicitors.

3 Delayed payments terms

We hope you will understand our position.

We are prepared to grant an extension.

We shall allow you an additional period of 12 days to make payment.

We would be prepared to accept a part/partial payment.

Your delay in payment is quite unacceptable.

4 Making and confirming payment

The invoice was mislaid.

We have instructed our bank to pay you the outstanding amount.

We have paid/transferred/remitted the sum of... to your account with the... Bank.

In settlement of your account/invoice...

We confirm receipt of your payment./We thank you for your (prompt) payment.

Your payment of... has been received by our bank.

documents against acceptance
C.O.D. (cash on delivery)
payment in advance
documentary letter of credit in your favour/favor
documentary bill of exchange
irrevocable and confirmed
documentary draft
payment on receipt of goods
at the current rate of exchange
payee
payable at the... bank

C Practising Language

1 Fill in the missing prepositions.

Dear Ms Foster

Thank you...[1] your letter...[2] 5th November and your cheque...[3] £1,000.00...[4] part settlement...[5] your account. But we would like to point out that the sum still outstanding is considerable.

As we work...[6] a great extent...[7] a small-profit basis, extended credit terms and the consequent loss...[8] interest tends to cancel out our profit.

...[9] the circumstances you will agree that long-term credit is impracticable. We would therefore appreciate your sending us a cheque...[10] the remaining sum...[11] £4,500.00 ...[12] return...[13] post.

We trust you will understand our position and look forward...[14] hearing...[15] you soon.

Yours sincerely

2 Complete the beginnings 1-10 with phrases a-h. Two of the items in 1-10 do not fit at all.

1 As requested we have credited your account
2 Despite our repeated requests for payment,
3 On going through our books we note
4 We are pleased to confirm
5 We request payment
6 Our invoice no.5647G
7 Your account still shows
8 We must now insist on
9 We would like to ask you
10 If we do not receive your remittance by 16 February.

a a debit balance of € 12,375.00.
b of the invoice total by 25 October.
c immediate settlement of our invoice.
d is still unpaid.
e we have received neither your payment nor an explanation for your failure to clear your account
f we shall have to consider taking legal steps
g with the amount of $756.00.
h that the payment of £1,275.69 clears your account.

3 Arrange these sentences in their proper order for a reminder.

a Any further delay in payment would wipe out our small profit altogether.

b But so far we have neither received payment nor did we have a letter explaining the reasons for your delay in settling our invoice.

c Dear Mr Raumer

d We have enslosed a copy of our invoice for your information.

e Therefore, we are all the more surprised and disappointed to find that you do not seem willing to fulfil your obligations.

f Two months ago we supplied you with a variety of buttons for the tourist trade in your region.

g We wrote to you asking for payment three weeks ago.

h We look forward to hearing from you by return.

i We went out of our way to ensure that the goods reached you promptly in time for the beginning of the tourist season.

j Claire Williams

k We would like to ask you to give this matter your immediate attention and clear your account promptly.

l You will understand that the products in question are low-margin articles.

m Yours sincerely.

Listening Comprehension

10 **4 Listen to this telephone conversation about a problem with the invoice.**

Role Play

5 Role-play the following telephone conversation with a partner.

A

- introduction, explains the problem, several items in recent invoice wrong
- gives required details
- refers to items 2, 5 and 8
- item 2: invoice price seems to be higher than list price; item 5: invoiced quantity is wrong (should be 25 instead of 52); item 8 was a special offer item, invoice price is identical with list price
- wants to know when he/she can expect a reply
- asks for the matter to be put right as quickly as possible

B

- introduction, asks how he/she can help
- asks for order number and date
- has got the invoice on the screen, asks which items are wrong
- asks for further details
- promises to settle the matter with the sales department, apologizes for the trouble
- promises to contact sales at once, thinks typing mistakes are the reason for the mistakes, hopes to phone back on the same day
- apologizes once again

D Writing letters

1 Use the phrases below to write a reminder to a long-standing customer.

Opening
- We refer to our statement for the first quarter which we sent you...
- Unfortunately, our account statement for the first quarter has not been settled yet.
- It may be possible that our statement for the first quarter has been overlooked.

Details
- We sent an account statement in early April and a note asking you to settle the outstanding amount in early May.
- So far, both our account statement from early April and our reminder of early May have gone/remained unanswered.

Action
- We must ask you to settle the outstanding amount without delay/by return.
- Unless you clear your account by (date) or offer a satisfactory explanation for the delay, we will have to consider (legal) steps to recover the outstanding amount.

Close
- We trust that you will settle your account in the next few days.
- If payment has already been made, please disregard this letter.

2 Summarize the letter and write a reply.

Wegener Kunststofftechnik GmbH
Wendenstr.87
31226 Peine

Germany

20 September 20..

Your order no. 9630/DW for hinges

Dear Mr Stolte

We refer to am. order and our invoice no. 24680, a copy of which is enclosed for your information. Your account has been in debit for more than eight weeks now.

An earlier request for the settlement of our invoice has remained unanswered and we have not received payment from you either.

You will understand that we are concerned about this situation. If you have any problems with meeting your commitments, we feel we should know about them so that we can work out a solution to your problem.

Please let us have some indication of how you are planning to proceed in this matter or, better still, transfer the full amount to clear your account.

We look forward to hearing from you in the near future.

Yours sincerely

Pamela Greer

Pamela Greer

(Accounts Dept.)

9 Complaints

Model letters: a complaint, reply to a complaint

Useful phrases: making a complaint (opening, saying that something has gone wrong, describing the damage, rejection of goods, solving the problem); dealing with complaints (replying to a complaint, accepting a complaint, rejecting a complaint)

Why make a complaint?

There are various reasons for making a complaint. The following are among the most frequent: delay in delivery, defective packing, wrong quality/quantity/colour/ measurements, faulty goods, discrepancies between invoice and goods delivered.

Exact details about the consignment (order no., number/type of goods) should be stated. The description of the fault must also be clear, precise and comprehensive. The buyer may suggest a solution to the problem. The tone of the letter must be friendly.

Having examined the statements made by the buyer, the seller will try to put the matter right or reject the buyer's claim. The seller will always keep the business relationship with the buyer in mind. For this reason, he will often look for a compromise solution, even if he is not to blame.

How to make and reply to complaints

	Complaint	Reply to a complaint
Opening	Refer to consignment/invoice, order and goods received.	Refer to the letter of complaint and apologise.
Details	State what is wrong and give exact details.	State the results of your investigation into the problem.

(Continued)

Terms	Ask for replacements or reduction of invoice amount. (Ask the supplier to take back unwanted goods.)	If the problem is your fault, offer a solution(replacement, reduction of invoice amount). If not, say why not. You may refer the buyer to the freight forwarder, insurance company, etc.)
Close	(Mention the urgency of the replacement consignment.) Close with a polite ending.	(Apologise again.) Close with a ploite ending.

A Model letters

1 A complaint

Style Limited

Fax *message*

62 Albert Sreet
London E1 5RT
Tel+44-(0)2-1724 9377
Fax+44-(0)2-1724 9388
Interne www.styfo.co.uk
Email info@styfo.co.uk

Textil Dorn GmbH
Karlstraβe 10
D-40593 Düsseldorf
Germany

22 April 20..

Order No. 9876/P for fine corduroy material

Dear Mr Dorn

Thank you for the consignment of fine corduroy material which we received yesterday.

Unfortunately, we have reason to complain. It seems that some of the colours do not quite match the samples you sent us earlier. This is especially true of the shades of green and bordeaux red (order Nos. 4673 and 4679) which we expected to be much lighter.

While we are prepared to keep all the other items ordered, we would like to ask you to check whether we were sent the right colours for items 8 and 10 of our order. If we have been sent the wrong goods, we would appreciate receiving replacement supplies as quickly as possible.

We will hold these two items at your disposal until we hear from you and will postpone settling your invoice until the matter has been clarified.

We look forward to hearing from you by return.

Yours sincerely

Jane Adams

Jane Adams

Buyer

Answer these questions.

1 When were the goods delivered?
2 What was wrong with the consignment?
3 Which order numbers does Ms Adams complain about?
4 What does Ms Adams ask Mr Dorn to do?
5 What is Ms Adams going to do with items 8 and 10?
6 Will the invoice be settled immediately?

2 Reply to a complaint

TextilDorn GmbH

Karlstr. 10 · D-40593 Düsseldorf
Telephone: +49-(0)211-78 34 11
Telefax: +49-(0)211-78 34 12
Email: info@textildorn.de
Internet: www.textildorn.de

F A X M E S S A G E

Style Four Limited
62 Albert Street
London El 5RT
England

Fax +44-(0)20-1724 9388

24 April 20..

Order No. 9876/P for fine corduroy material

Dear Ms Adams

Thank you for your fax message. We are sorry to read that you were not happy with the colours of the corduroy materials we sent you. We have looked into the matter very carefully and can only confirm that the colours you were sent are those that you ordered.

There may be a very simple explanation to the discrepancy in shades that you noticed. Certain colours tend to fade when exposed to strong light over a longer period. This may have occurred with the samples we sent you. We apologise for this but it certainly was not our intention to mislead you in any way.

To avoid disappointment we would, by way of exception, be willing to take back items 8 and 10. You must be aware, however, that we can not send you the lighter colouring that you prefer.

If you do not want to keep the items in question, please return them to us carriage forward. Otherwise, please settle our invoice as agreed.

We hope you can agree to this solution and look forward to hearing from you.

Yours sincerely

Jens Dorn

Jens Dorn

B Useful phrases

1 Making a complaint

Opening

We received your consignment of... yesterday which we had ordered on... /The consignment... reached us yesterday.

Your consignment of... was delivered yesterday (as advised).

(We)Thank you foryour consignment of... which arrived here/which we received yesterday.

Saying that something has gone wrong

Unfortunately, there has been an error in the handling/execution of our order No. ...

The goods sent/delivered are not the ones we had ordered.

The quality of the goods did not meet/did not come up to our expectations.

Describing the damage

You sent us 500... instead of the 250 which we had ordered.

The contents of the crates do not agree with the packing list/delivery note.

The goods are not the colour/size we ordered/... were faulty.

Article number... was missing from the consignment.

Several of the items were scratched/ broken/(slightly) damaged.

The goods seem to have been badly packed.

Rejection of goods

We cannot accept the goods for these reasons.

We must ask you to send us (a) replacement(s) as soon as possible.

We are returning part of the/the whole consignment.

Solving the problem

We are prepared to keep the goods (at a reduced price of... per article/item).

We can only sell the damaged goods at a considerably reduced price.

We must now cancel our/the order.

We must ask for/insist on compensation to cover our losses.

We must ask you to credit us with the value of the damaged goods.

This has caused us considerable difficulties/inconvenience with a number of customers.

2 Dealing with complaints

Replying to a complaint

We are sorry to hear that you have had reason to complain about...

We have checked your complaint.

As the damage happened in transit,...

Accepting a complaint

We offer you our sincere apologies for this error.

We are prepared to exchange/replace the goods for/with some of a similar quality.

We shall replace the goods at our expense.

We are prepared to offer you a reduction of... %.

Rejecting a complaint

We have checked the goods very carefully and can find no fault with the goods.

We cannot accept responsibility for the damage.

We regret that we cannot take the goods back.

We must point out that the period of guarantee has expired.

C Practising language

1 **Use 20 of the 23 verbs from the box to fill in the missing verbs in the correct form in the sentences below.**

arrive | be | be afraid | be broken | be damaged | be missing | cause check | complain | ensure | find | not agree | not be packed | not match notice | open | order | pay | receive | return | see | send | understand

1 We... you... us the wrong goods.
2 The contents of case 7... with the packing list.
3 We... 500 sweaters, but only... 250.
4 When we... the consignment, we... that the jeans... of the wrong sizes.
5 Unfortunately, the material... the samples.
6 When we... the case, we... that item 6 from our order...
7 Some of the china... because the goods... sufficiently well.
8 We... no alternative but to... the goods to you.
9 Please... that the replacement goods... in time for the fair.
10 You... that the delay in delivery... us considerable inconvenience.

2 **Complete the sentence beginnings 1-8 with the appropriate phrases a-j. Two of the phrases in a-j don't fit at all.**

1 We accept responsibility for the damage
2 We are prepared to keep the goods
3 Your failure to supply the goods on time has caused us
4 Unfortunately, we have reason to complain
5 We have to ask for compensation
6 We offer our sincere apologies
7 In the circumstances, we are, of course, prepared to replace the goods
8 We suggest that you report the matter

a about a delay in delivery.
b at a substantially reduced price.
c at our expense.
d which must have occurred in transit.
e the consignment which arrived yesterday.
f for this error.
g to cover our losses.
h to your insurance company.

i considerable inconvenience with our customers.
j instead of 100 items.

3 The sentence parts below are in the wrong order. Rearrange them to form meaningful sentences. Add commas where necessary.

1 On examining/some of them/that / the articles/we discovered/were damp
2 After operating the machine/as expected/ for a short time/we noticed/ it did not perform/that
3 as proof/enclosed/For your information/of the damage/please find/some photos
4 goods/It goes/of this quality / that/to our customers/we cannot offer/ without saying
5 but/have arrived/no alternative/the replacement goods/to delay payment/ until/ We have
6 and expense/at your risk/In the circumstances/the faulty goods/to return/ we have decided
7 ask you/can be done/right / therefore / to let us know / to put the matter/ We must/what
8 by at least 20 per cent/if you reduce/only be prepared/the price/ to keep the goods/We will

4 Describe the charts.

As a member of a sales team, you have been involved in a survey of customer satisfaction. Your head of department is to present the two charts below at a meeting of sales directors of an international group. Describe the results of the survey as shown in the charts.

Chart 1 Comptaints

Chart 2 **Customer satisfaction ratio** (in percentage of respondents)

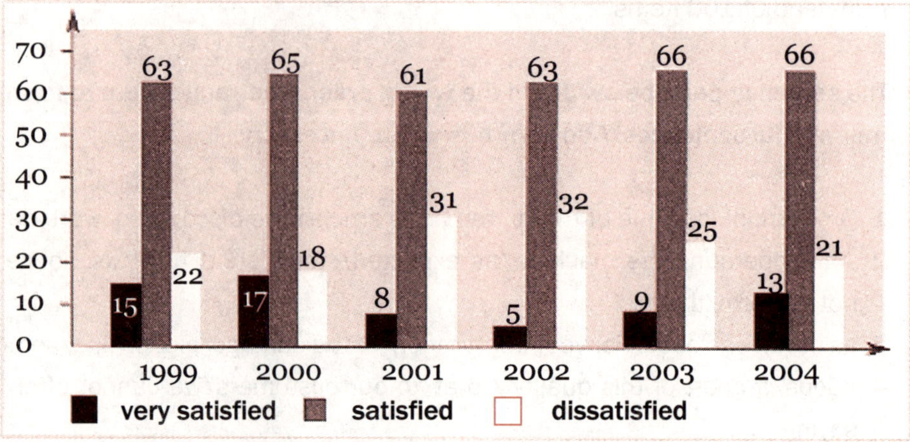

Listening Comprehension

11 5 **Listen to this telephone conversation about a problem with an invoice.**

Draft an email to Helen (in English) and briefly summarize the main points of the telephone conversation.

D Writing letters

1 **Summarize the letter and write a complaint.**

Your order for washing machines no. 1357/TS

Dear Mr Wolters

Thank you for your fax about the above-mentioned order. We were disappointed to read that some of the machines arrived scratched and that the plastic foil and cardboard covering were damaged and torn. We are now looking into the matter and have contacted our shipping company. You will understand that it will take us some time to find out how the damage could have happened. We would very much appreciate it if you could let us have a few more days to investigate the matter.

From your description of the damage and the photographs you sent us, however, it would seem that this problem may have been because of rough handling rather than poor packing. We have not had customers complain about inadequate packing before. In our opinion, such damage can only have occurred after the goods left our premises. We are now waiting for the shipping company's report and will contact you as soon as we receive it.

We are, of course, sorry that this happened at all and are confident that the matter will be settled to the satisfaction of all parties concerned.

In the meantime, we have despatched replacement machines as you need them urgently to meet your customers' orders and hope that they will arrive in good order and condition.

We will contact you again as soon as we have the shipping company's report.

Yours sincerely

Chris Bulmer
(Despatch Manager)

2 Write a reply to this fax.

James Murray Textiles & Trading Ltd
Humberstone Business Park
18 Jameson Street
Bradford
BD6 3OP

30June20..

Order No. 4567/D

Dear Ms Clark

We are sorry to report that the consignment of cotton shirts despatched on 26 June (our order No. 4567/D) was delivered to us yesterday in a very unsatisfactory state. It was clear that two Of the cases (Nos. 4 & 7) had been tampered with. Case No.4 contained only 468 shirts and case No. 7 only 475 instead of the five hundred invoiced for each. Before taking the matter up with our forwarding agent, we would be grateful if you could confirm that each of these cases contained the invoiced quantity when they left your warehouse in Ashstead. At the same time, we would like you to replace the fifty-seven missing shirts with others of the same quality.

We look forward to your reply.

Yours sincerely
Anke Solms
Anke Solms

3 Write two emails from notes.

See the following details to write two replies to this email.

Dear Sylvia

We have just received and unpacked your consignment of leather belts from our order no. 7788-DA (dated 12 January). As I couldn't get you on the phone, I'm writing this message and hope you'll be able to read it soon.

On checking the packing list and comparing it with our order, we noticed that there seem to be some discrepancies in quantities and sizes. Could I ask you to check whether there have been any mistakes and let me know as soon as possible? We really need to get our ranges ready and out to our customers very quickly now.

Hope to read your reply soon.

Best

Joanne

10 Applying for a job

Model letters: letter of application, CV

Useful phrases: referring to the source of information; applying foravacancy; giving information; motivation for the new job; closing sentences

The parts of a job application

A job application is usually made up of several parts:

- the cover(ing) letter or letter of application,
- the CV (curriculum vitae) or résumé or personal data sheet (PDS) and
- certificates and testimonials (unusual in Britain or the U.S.A.).

An application can be either **solicited** (the applicant replies to a job advertisement) or **unsolicited** (the applicant acts on his/her own initiative).

The cover letter and the CV are the applicant's most important selling tools. Recruiters often shortlist candidates on the basis of the information provided in these documents. Therefore they should give comprehensive information about the person, the quailfications, experience and skills of the job applicant.

How to write a letter of application

The cover letter should not be longer than about 20 lines. It has four parts:

Opening	Solicited application: refer to the job advertisement and say which job you are applying for. Unsolicited application: refer to recently obtained qualification or state reason for intended job change. Say which iob you are applying for.
Qualifications and skills	State the qualifications, skills and experience that make you particularly suitable for the jab.
Motivation	Write why you are applying and what you hope to achieve in the new post.
Close	State that further information can be given if necessary and when you are available for an interview. Say that you would appreciate a positive reply.

How to write a CV

The CV gives a full account of the candidate's education, qualifications and experience. It should be no longer than one page. Note: Unlike German CVs, a photo is not included in the UK or in the U.S.A.. There are usually five sections in the CV:

1 Personal data	Give your address, telephone number and email address, as well as personal information: age (or date and place of birth). To prevent discrimination, there is very little personal information (i.e. regarding sex, marital status, religion) in British or American CVs.
2 Education	Give details of your school career and your college or university qualifications. State subjects and grade in final exam.
3 Job/Work experience	State where and when you trained for a job. Mention work experience including practicals or internships.
4 Skills and activities	State other qualifications and skills that may be helpful in your job (languages, IT skills, training courses relevant for the job, interests and spare time activities).
5 References	British and American CVs usually have the following sentence at the bottom of the page: "References supplied (up) on request". This is because employers do not normally write lengthy testimonials about an employee's work and abilities. Instead, they usually give a reference when asked. The applicant will give the address if necessary.

Note: CVs are not signed or dated. They often provide the information in reverse chronological order, i.e. starting with the most recent events and then going back.

A Model letters and CVs

1 Letter of application

Timo Sanders writes a cover letter for his application for a work placement.

Timo Sanders

Alte Landstr. 17
45875 Gelsenkirchen
Tel. 02 09/48 62 48
mobile: 0160/27 34 987
email: timosandersl@gmx.de

Northumberland Farm Supplies Ltd
Morpeth Branch
17 North Morpeth Business Park
Morpeth
Northumberland
NE62 4RD
England

12 January 20..

Application for a work placement

Dear Sir or Madam

A work placement abroad is strongly recommended for students of business administration at the Gelsenkirchen Polytechnic. Therefore, I am planning to do such a placement during the summer break this year and would like to ask you to consider my application for a three-month placement in your company.

I obtained your address from the WCG (a farm supplies distributor) here in where I completed a vocational training of two and a half years before taking up business administration at Gelsenkirchen Polytechnic. As I am familiar with the trade of products for the farming community here in Germany, I would like to gain experience in a similar field in Britain.

As you will see from the enclosed CV, I am a fully qualified Management Assistant in Wholesale and Foreign Trade. I am able to familiarise myself with computer applications very quickly and have a good command of English. Business English is an integral component of our degree course.

If possible, I would like to join your firm for the summer months, ideally for the period from 1 July to 30 September, but other periods would also be possible. Should you have any further queries, please do not hesitate to contact me by phone or mail.

I would be pleased to be able to work in Morpeth and look forward to your reply.

Yours faithfully

Time Sanders

Enclosures

Answer these questions.

1 What are students of business administration expected to do?

2 For how long does Timo plan to go to Britain?

3 What did Timo do at the WCG for two and a half years?

4 What qualification did Timo get at the end of his training?

5 How good is Timo's English?

6 When is Timo planning to come to Britain?

2 CV

Here is the CV that Timo sends together with the cover letter.

Timo Sanders

Alte Landstr. 17
45875 Gelsenkirchen
Tel. 02 09/48 62 48
mobile: 0160/27 34 987
email: timosanders 1@gmx.de

Curriculum vitae

PERSONAL DATA

Born:	31 October 1981 in Bremen
Nationality:	German
Marital status:	Single

EDUCATION

1987-1991	Primary school in Bremen
1991-1997	Comprehensive school in Bremen School-leaving certificate (corresponds to GCSE)
1997-1999	College of Commerce in Münster Fachabitur (corresponds to A-levels) Average grade: 2.3
Since 2001	Gelsenkirchen Polytechnic 4-yearcourse in Business Management

WORK EXPERIENCE

1998-1999	WCG Münster—part-time work (assisting in the warehouse)
1999-2001	WCG Münster—vocational training as Management Assistant in Wholesale and Foreign Trade
Spring 2001	Qualifying examination for Management Assistant in Wholesale and Foreign Trade at the Münster Chamber of Commerce and Industry (IHK) Final grade: 1.7 (89%)

ACTIVITIES AND QUALIFICATIONS

2001-2002	Community service (meals-on-wheels unit of the local Red Cross branch)
Languages	English—good (some knowledge of business English)

	French—fair
	Spanish—beginner
Computer literacy	Familiar with standard software programs (MS Office, Lotus, Linux)
Activities	Handball, also coaching a bays' team at C-level
	Member of the Gelsenkirchen Polytechnic student representative council

References can be supplied upon request.

B Useful phrases

1 Referring to the source of information

I have learned from the job centre/careers office that you are recruiting... /have a vacancy for...

You advertised the post/position of ... in yesterday's/today's issue/in the issue of... of...

I was interested to read your advertisement in last week's edition of the...

2 Applying for a vacancy

I wish to apply/I would like you to consider my application for the advertised post.

Following our telephone conversation/As discussed on the phone today, I am sending you my application.

Having completed my training/university course in... , I am now looking for a post in...

3 Giving information

As you will see from the enclosed curriculum vitae/resume/profile,...

I am currently working for an import firm /as a foreign language correspondent in a wholesaling company.

I am computer-literate./I have a lot of experience in customer services.

I speak fluent English and Spanish/English and Spanish fluently and have a basic knowledge of French.

I have qualifications/a diploma/a degree in...

... where I studied. ... as my main subject [US: my major] (and... as my subsidiary subject [US: my minor]).

... I graduated in the following subjects:...

After my (vocational) training, I worked for a local export firm for four years.

During my studies, I did two work placements/practicals abroad.

I was trained as a bilingual/foreign-language secretary.

4 Motivation for the new job

I am looking for as similar post with more responsibility/promotion prospects.

I hope to/I am confident that I will be able to use/apply my skills/experience in... in the advertised post.

I have taken a great interest in working (together) with... during my training.

I now wish to change my job/to work for a larger organisation.

I wish to work abroad and to make use of my knowledge of languages.

5 Closing sentences

You will find my CV and copies of my diplomas/certificates enclosed.

Should you require further information about my person or my qualifications, I would be pleased to quote references.

The names of two referees [US: references] are given below.

I am available for an interview at any time.

I would be grateful for/appreciate the opportunity to present myself in an interview.

C Practising language

1 Decide which does not fit into the group.

1	**a** receptionist	**b** telephonist	**c** stockist	**d** typist
2	**a** accounts manager	**b** human resources manager	**c** personnel officer	**d** recruiter
3	**a** buying clerk	**b** chief buyer	**c** purchasing manager	**d** warehouse manager
4	**a** advertising agent	**b** product manager	**c** sales assistant	**d** sales representative
5	**a** deputy manager	**b** office clerk	**c** personal assistant	**d** secretary
6	**a** builder	**b** fitter	**c** maintenance engineer	**d** technician

2 Replace the terms in *italics* by suitable ones from the box below. There are more terms than you need.

a candidate | activities | advertisement | available | believe | challenging
completing | continued | customers | department | experience | helpful
interest | interview | issue | references | standard | testimonials | training

I was interested to see your *announcement*[1] for the post of a junior export sales officer in the June *copy*[2] of "Trade International" and I would like to be considered as *an applicant*[3] for that vacancy.

I *feel*[4] I am fully qualified for the post as after *ending*[5] my course in business studies at Kingston College of Further Education,I worked in the sales *section*[6] of a small local wholesale business. My *tasks*[7] there involved dealing with *business contacts*[8] at home and abroad. I am familiar with the *traditional* [9] office communication facilities. At college, I *carried on* with[10] French and also learnt some Spanish.

I am keen to do some more *demanding*[11] work and feel that the experience gained in my present job will be *useful* [12] in your company.

My CV and the usual *certificates*[13] are enclosed.

I am *ready*[14] for a personal *discussion*[15] at your convenience and look forward to hearing from you.

3 Reorganise the parts in the proper order to form full sentences. Choose the correct forms of the verbs.

1 as a management assistant/I/in human resources/train with/Wolters Maschinenbau GmbH
2 as an assistant to the area sales manager/for two years/I/in Swansea/work
3 additional courses/as a management assistant in insurance/attend/during my training/I / to improve my computing skills
4 as a management assistant/complete/in property management/in two months' time/I /my training
5 as a temp/I/in the logistics department/of IPEX Mediatechnik GmbH/since leaving school/work
6 as a management assistant/in wholesaling and retailing/last/my training/three years
7 for an opening in an engineering company/having completed/I/in office communication/look/my training
8 after my traineeship/continue/I/in the capacity of field representative/to work/with Steinmeyer & Partners/with this company

4 Use the ideas in brackets to complete these sentences.

1 The advertisement on your website for the post of bilingual sales manager... (*interest me*)
2 I am interested in applying for the advertised vacancy and... (*enclose personal profile*)
3 As an experienced administrative assistant,... (*meet requirements*)
4 I believe that I have the necessary drive and team spirit... (*contribute to business success*)

5 My present job involves a lot of keyboarding activities.Therefore,... (*familiarity with word processing software*)
6 Having gained experience in a small but busy office,... (*seek new challenge*)
7 I feel that, with my foreign language skills,... (*contribute to international sales efforts)*
8 I would welcome the opportunity... (*come for an interview*)
9 Should you require any further information,... (*phone or mail*)
10 If necessary... (*supply references*)

5 **Rewrite the following cover letter to avoid the repetition of *I*-structures. Go back to the Useful phrases section (Part B of this Unit) and read the suggestions in the box below for ideas.**

- Having graduated...
- Having seen...
- In the position of... ,I...
- In your advertisement...
- That is why/Therefore I...
- You can reach me...
- You can see...

Application for post of PA

I saw your advertisement for the post of PA in yesterday's issue of the *New York Times.*

I would like to apply for this post and am sending you my CV as an enclosure.

I am confident that I meet your requirements as I have recently graduated from Albany Secretarial College. I have good keyboarding skills (50 wpm) and shorthand skills (40 wpm). I gained some experience as a secretary at Ogilvy&Partners (a law firm) where I did a lot of copy-typing.

I am now seeking a new challenge in an office with more direct client contact and more responsible work. I would like to make better use of the foreign language skills I acquired at school and in evening classes. I am also familiar with the standard software programs. I would very much enjoy becoming part of an active team-oriented environment.

I will be happy to supply any supplementary information you require and am available for an interview at any time.

I can be contacted by phone or email and I look forward to your reply.

Role Play

6 Interview your partner.

In a job interview, the interviewee is usually asked about points like career at school/ university, job training, work experience, special skills and previous employers.

a **Think of questions the interviewer might ask. Consider some of the following points:**

- school qualifications
- stays abroad (where, for how long)
- skills other than those acquired at school, e.g. language or IT
- job training (special area, where, how long, which company department, job content)
- company profile (type of company, size, product range, markets)

b **With a partner, role-play an interview for a job.**

Interviewer: Use some of the points raised in **a** above to find out as much about your partner as you can. Try to follow a logical sequence but also take up points made by the interviewee.

Interviewee: Use your own personal profile to answer the interviewer's questions. Give more detailed information whenever suitable.

Listening Comprehension

12 **7 Listen to the telephone message and take notes. Pass the information on to your neighbour.**

Sheila takes a telephone message for her brother Roger and tells him about an appointment for an interview when he comes home later in the evening. Write a note to Roger including the following details:

- who called and why
- contact details
- information about the appointment and where to go

D Writing letters and CVs

1 Decide which of the terms and expressions in *italics* are suitable for a cover letter. Work in groups.

1 I was interested to see your *advertisement/announcement/commercial/information* [a]*for the job/place/post/position* [b] of an event manager and I *plan/want/wish/would like* [c] to *apply/be considered/be chosen/stand* as a candidate [d].

2 As you will *see/note/notice/remark* [a] from my *CV/factsheet/profile/resume* [b], I have the *asked for/demanded/necessary/required* [d]*certificates/exams/qualifications/tests* [c] to meet your *claims/demands/requests/requirements* [e].

3 After *attending/going to/leaving/visiting* [a] *driving school/college/university/the polytechnic* [b] *I learnt the job of / studied the work of / trained as/was educated as* [c] a singer.

4 I *gained/had/made/obtained* [a] *some experience/information/knowledge/skills* [b] in an advertising *agency/company/bureau/company/office* [c] and I would now like to *get to know/to know/to learn about/to see* [d] the *function/job/task/work* [e] of a public relations *branch/department/office/section* [f].

5 *If/Should/When/Whenever* [a] you require *additional/better/further/more* [b] information, please do not hesitate to *call/contact/inform/tell* [c] me.

2 Put these sentences in the proper order for a cover letter.

Dear Mr Henderson,

a An interview can be arranged at anytime.

b I will have completed my two-year training as an office assistant with Hunters Corp here in Portland by the end of June.

c But as my company has no opening for me, I am now looking for opportunities to use my skills elsewhere.

d During mytraineeship, I also attended evening classes in office management, computing and general secretarial duties.

e You will see from my resume and certificates that I have already gained some work experience in the sector in which you operate.

f I am confident that my training and the skills I acquired at college make me suitable for such a position.

g I found your address in the career centre's job file and wish to apply for the advertised post of junior office assistant.

h I look forward to hearing from you.

i If you require any additional information, please do not hesitate to contact me by phone or mail.

j I hope to gain further experience and to make a positive contribution to the success of your business.

Yours truly,

3 Reassemble the information below for a CV.

Use the following headings:

Personal data; Education ; Work experience; Activities and interests.

1990-1993 Primary school in Munich

1993-2002 Grammar school in Munich, Abitur (average grade 2.3)

1999-2000 6 months exchange visit to Seaford sixth form college

2002-present Traineeship at Hypo-und Vereinsbank (HVB) in Munich

80021 Munich

Born on 21 November 1984 in Kempten

Christina Voigt

Computer literacy

Curriculum vitae

E-Mail tinavoigt@t-online.de

English—fluent

July 2001 1 month's work experience at Barclay's Bank London—customer services department

Familiar with standard software programs

Female

French—fairly fluent

Interests

Languages

Reading, riding, travelling, meeting people

References supplied upon request

Robert-Koch-Str.15

Single

Tel. 089/49 50 819

4 Applying for a job in a temping agency.

Refer to your telephone conversation with someone from a temping agency and write a cover letter for your application for one of these office jobs.

Positions	Requirements
Executive assistant	1 year office experience
Legal assistant	MS Office skills
Bilingual secretary	foreign languages
Receptionist	friendly personality
	good communicative skills
	able to work under pressure

5 **Write a cover letter and a CV.**

Write a cover letter and CV based on your own personal profile (school career, work experience, activities, skills, interests) to apply for a 3-month work placement in a field of your choice.

Glossary

A

(account) statement
A-levels[GB]
accept an invitation
accept responsibility for
accounting
accounting error
accurate
acknowledgement/confirmation of (an) order
additional
addressee
adequate stock levels
adjust a mistake
advantageous
advertise
advertisement
advice of dispatch/shipment, delivery/ advice note
advise/inform sb
agenda
agent
amend an invoice
amendment
amount
amount due/owing, outstanding sum/
apologise
application
apply for a job/vacancy/post
apprentice
apprenticeship
arrange
arrange a date
arrange for delivery to be made
as agreed
as far as... goes/is concerned
as per
at your convenience
at your expense
authorise

B

batch, shipment, consignment
be based on
be beyond one's control
be computer-literate
be desperate for
be dissatisfied with
be grateful
be in stock
be interested in
be obliged
be out of stock
be overdue
be one's fault
be tied up
be to blame
be willing
below list (price)
Best wishes
binding/firm
branch
brochure, leaflet
bulk/volume order
business dealings
business matters
business relationship

buyer's guide
by air
by air mail
by express, special delivery
by rail
by road
by sea
by separate post, under separate cover
by way of compensation (for)
by way of exception

C

cancel an order
carbon copy, copy circulated
carrier
cash discount
cash with order (CWO)
catalogue
certificate
chain
chamber of commerce
charge
clarify
clear an account
compensation
competitive offer
competitive prices
competitive situation
complain about
complaint
compliance with (the law)
conditions
conference facilities
conference room
confirm a hotel reservation
confirm an appointment
conform to
consignor, shipper, sender
contract of sale
counteroffer
cover one's losses
credit
credit note
custom-made/customised
customer
CV (curriculum vitae), résumé, personal data sheet (PDS)

D

damaged
deadline for payment
Dear Sir or Madam
debit
debit balance
debit note
defective packing
delay in delivery
delay in payment
delayed payment terms
delivery (requirements)
delivery commitments
delivery date
delivery period
delivery schedule
delivery terms, terms of delivery
delivery/dispatch note
delivery; shipment/ consignment
demonstrate, present
depend on
details
discount
discrepancy
dispatch, make delivery
distribution
distributor
do business with sb
double room

E

edition, issue

enclosed
enclosure
enquiry
ensure
evaluate
examination
examine
exceed a credit period
execution of order
export
extend (a range)
extended credit terms, long-term credit

F

fair
faulty goods
finalise
finish, workmanship
fix a date
follow-up order
for display purposes
for inspection
for our files
for the attention of
for/on behalf of
forthcoming
forward
forward carriage/on-carriage
forwarding/shipping agent, freight forwarder
franco domicile
free delivery and transport
fulfil/meet our requirements
further to

G

gain experience
get in touch with sb, to contact sb
(general) terms and conditions of business
go unnoticed
good command of a language
goods
graduate in
grant an extension
gross (price)
guarantee

H

handling
hold at one's disposal

I

identify goods
if possible
importer
in due course
in good orde rand condition
in small print
in the week commencing...
in transit
inconvenience
inconvenient
initial order
instructions for shipment/ dispatch
insurance
interview
introductory discount
introductory offer
investigate/look into a matter
invitation
invite
invite sb for an interview
invoice
irrevocable and confirmed letter of credit
IT (information technology) skills, computer literacy
it is agreed

J

job application

(job) interview

L

late delivery
launch
leading
legal action
let sb know
line

M

make a hotel reservation
make an appointment
make to customer's specifications
Management Assistant in Wholesale and Foreign Trade
manufacture
manufacturer
market
marketing
marketing manager
means of transport
meanwhile
meet one's (financial) obligations/commitments
meet one's requirements
model number
mutual (customer)

N

negotiate
net (price)

O

off-the-shelf product
offer
offer a reduction
on a strict rota basis
on sale or return
order form
order handling/processing
order number
outlet
overhead projector
overlook

P

pack
packing list
packing, packaging
padding material
palletise
part/partial payment
payment on delivery (P/D)
period of guarantee
plant
post code, ZIP code
postpone
postpone an appointment
premises
price list
principal
prior engagement
process/execute an order
product line
production volume
provide sb with
provided that
purchasing
purchasing manager
put a matter right

Q

quarterly statement
query an invoice
quotation
quote a delivery date
quote a price

R

range
ready for dispatch/shipment
recommend
recommendation
record
reference
registered mail
registered name
registration number
reject a complaint/claim
relate to
remainder/remaining amount/sum, balance
reminder, collection letter
remittance, transfer
repeat order
replace goods
replacement
replacement consignment/supply
request for payment
reserve the right
retail outlet
return if undelivered
revise
revised discounts/prices
revised terms
(road) haulier, haulage company

S

safety regulations
sales material/literature
sample, specimen
satisfactory
scratched
secretary/PA (personal assistant)
self-addressed/stamp-addressed envelope
settle an invoice
settlement (of invoice)
settlement of an invoice
ship
shipment, consignment
shipper
shipping space
sign
signature block
single room
skills
solicitor
special terms
stand (at a trade fair)
stellen to charge
stipulate
stores
strictly adhere to
subject to confirmation
submit
substandard, inferior
suitable
summer collection
supplier
supply
supply an address/a reference
supply contract
supply from stock
supply information
surcharge

T

take a matter up with sb
take the opportunity
tally with
tamper with sth
tax
technical data sheet
terms of payment and delivery
terms of payment/ business
terms of the offer
testimonial, reference

testing purposes
time allowed for payment
(to do an) internship, a placement
to meet one's expectations
to put sb under pressure
to suggest a date
top-quality
torn
trade discount
trainee
traineeship
transfer, remit
transport arrangements
travel arrangements/plans
trial order
tunnel terminal

U

undersigned
urgency
urgent

V

(vocational) qualification
(vocational) training
valid
video projector
volume discount

W

warranty, guarantee
well-established
(work) experience
wholesale
wholesaler
with reference to
within a fortnight of receipt of

Y

Yours faithfully
Yours sincerely

A-Z Word List

A

B

C

Transcripts

2 Unit 2 Exercise A1

Lisa: *Guten Morgen. UB Consult GmbH. Lisa Schmitz. Was kann ich für Sie tun?*

Sam: *Oh, good morning. Uhm...Look, do you mind if I speak English, please?*

Lisa: *Not at all.Go ahead.*

Sam: *Thanks. Can I speak to Ms Bach, please?*

Lisa: *Of course. Who's calling, please?*

Sam: *My name's Kavanagh, Sam Kavanagh.*

Lisa: *Could you spell that for me, please?*

Lisa: *Sorry, is that G for Golf and H for Hotel?*

Sam: *Yes, that's right, but we don't pronounce them.*

Lisa: *Okay, I've got that. Could you hold the line, please, Mr Kavanagh?I'll put you through.*

Sam: *Thanks a lot. (pause with music)*

Lisa: *Hello? Mr Kavanagh?*

Lisa: *I'm so sorry, but Ms Bach's not in her offce. She had to go out, I'm afraid. Can I take a message for her?*

Sam: *Yes. Can you ask her to ring me, please? The number's 00353 for Ireland, then 91 for Galway, then 572231.*

Lisa: *I've got that. International code 00353, then 91572231, right?*

Sam: *That's right. Oh, and could you tell her it's quite urgent, please? I' m away for the rest of the week.*

Lisa: *Okay. I'll make sure she has your message as soon as she gets back.*

Sam: *Thanks very much. Goodbye.*

Lisa: *Bye now, Mr Kavanagh.*

3 Unit 2 Exercise A2

Lisa: *Guten Tag. UB Consult GmbH. Was kann ich für Sie tun?*

Kate: *Lisa? It's Kate Connors here.*

Lisa: *Oh, hello, Kate. How're you?*

Kate: *Fine, thanks, Lisa. And you?*

Lisa: *I'm fine, too, thanks. Now, what can I do for you?*

Kate: *Well, I'm just calling to fix a date and time for Sam's meeting with Mr and Mrs Bach at the Ispo Sportmode fair in Munich next month.*

Lisa: *Oh, yes. Just a moment, Kate. Mr Bach gave me some dates and times.*
(pause).
Kate?

Kate: *Yes?*

Lisa: *Well, how about Saturday, the first at nine-thirty? That's on the first day of the fair.*

Kate: *Oh, that's just fine, Lisa. Sam's free then. Now, did Mr Bach say anything about the venue?*

Lisa: *Well,Mr Bach has booked a room for Saturday morning. Could you ask Mr Kavanagh to go to room eight on the first floor of the small* *conference centre near the entrance to the exhibition ground?*

Kate: *Oh, dear. Where was that, Lisa?*

Lisa: *Well, the small conference centre is just inside the Theresienhöhe entrance to the exhibition ground. But that shouldn't be a problem. Everything's very well signed in German and English.*

Kate: *Fine, I've got that, I think, but let me just check—nine-thirty on the first of February in room eight on the first floor of the conference centre at the Theresienhö he entrance to the exhibition ground, right?*

Lisa: *That's right, but I'll email to confirm anyhow. Well, thanks for calling, Kate, and please tell Mr Kavanagh that Mr and Mrs Bach are looking very forward to meeting him.*

Kate: *I'll certainly do that. Well, take care, Lisa. Goodbye.*

Lisa: *Bye now,Kate.*

4 Unit 2 Exercise C6

Jane: *Good afternoon. Carr & Sons Limited. Can I help you?*

Ben: *Good afternoon. Can you put me through to Ms King's office, please?*

Jane: *Certainly. Who's calling, please?*

Ben: *My name's Ben Todd.*

Jane: *Hold the line, please, Mr Todd.*

Ann: *Good afternoon. Ms King's office. Ann Johnson speaking.*

Ben: *Good afternoon. It's Ben Todd here. May I speak to Ms King, please?*

Ann: *I m sorry. I' m afraid Ms King is in a meeting at the moment.*

Ben: *Oh, dear. Do you know when she'll be free? I'll call again later.*

Ann: *Well, I'm afraid I don't know when the meeting will be over. But can I take a message?*

Ben: *Oh no, thank you. It's private. I' d rather send an email. Thank you. Bye.*

Ann: *Goodbye.*

5 Unit 3 Exercise C6

Kim: *Good morning. Star Car Hire. I'm Kim Cameron. Can I help you?*

Joe: *Hi. My name's Joe Davis. Look, I've a question first. Is it possible to hire a car from Aberdeen Dyce airport but return it at Glasgow Airport?*

Kim: *No problem,sir.There's a Star office at all Scottish airports.*

Joe: *Fine. In that case, what would a car cost for five days, please?*

Kim: *What class of car are you thinking of, sir? We have five groups from a VWPolo or a Ford Fiesta in Group A through to luxury limousines in Group E.*

Joe: *Well, the car's not for me, actually. It's for my boss. But I know she wants to do a lot of touring, so the car should be comfortable. She doesn't want anything luxurious, though.*

Kim: *In that case, I'd suggest Group C, sir. What about an Audi A4 or a Peugeot 307, for example?*

Joe: *The Peugeot sounds good. She drives a Peugeot herself. How much is the 307, then?*

Kim: *Well, that depends on the day of the week. Weekends are much cheaper.*

Joe: *Well, she wants to pick the car up at nine am on Monday, the sixteenth of March at Dyce and return it at six pm on Friday, the twentieth at Glasgow Airport.*

Kim: *Thanks. So that's Group C for four days and nine hours during the week. Just a moment, please. Er... that's two hundred and eleven pounds ninety-nine.*

Joe: *Good heavens.That's a lot, isn't it? Does that price include a full tank of petrol?*

Kim: *No, it doesn't, sir. The tank's full when you pick up the car, of course, but you have to give it back with a full tank as well. If you don't, you have to pay a ten pound surcharge in addition to the cost of our filling the tank, I'm afraid.*

Joe: *I see. Are there any other extras?*

Kim: *No. Petrol is the only extra. The price includes full insurance and unlimited mileage.*

Joe: *Ah, so there's no mileage surcharge?*

Kim: *No, sir—and that's important if you're touring.*

Joe: *Okay, then. Look, can I get back to you later? I'm sure it'll be okay, but I'd better check with my boss before making a firm reservation.*

Kim: *Sure. No problem, sir. We're open at Dyce until 10 pm, by the way.*

Joe: *Fine. Well, thanks for your help. Bye now.*

Kim: *You're welcome. Goodbye, sir.*

6 Unit 4 Exercise A1

Pia: *Guten Morgen. Textil Dorn. Pia Marx am Apparat.*

Jane: *Oh,...Is there anyone I can talk to who speaks English, please?*

Pia: *Of course. How can I help you?*

Jane: *Well, my name's Jane Adams from Style Four in London. I'd like to speak to somebody in export, please.*

Pia: *Well, we don't have a separate export department, I'm afraid. I'll put you through to Mr Dorn.*

(pause)

Dorn: *Dorn.*

Jane: *Oh, good morning, Mr Dorn. My name's Jane Adams from Style Four in London.*

Dorn: *Good morning, Ms Adams. What can I do for you?*

Jane: *Well, we're looking for denim cloth for our new line in jeans. Do you supply that kind of material?*

Dorn: *Yes, we do. We act as European agents for a number of* manufacturers. What are you looking for exactly?

Jane: *Well, at the moment we're interested in high-quality light stretch denim in various colours for our summer collection. Can you help us there?*

Dorn: *Yes, we can. We can offer an excellent range of Italian denim at very competitive prices, for example.*

Jane: *That sounds interesting. Could you send us samples in various colours?*

Dorn: *Of course. We can send you our standard collection of samples and then we can take it from there.*

Jane: *Thank you. I'll fax you the details. (...)*

7 Unit 5 Exercise C5

Pat: *Good morning. Wessex Fitness Technology. Pat King speaking.*

Jo: *Hi. It's Top Fit Studios in Southport here. I'm calling about our enquiry for digital...*

Pat: *Sorry, can we take it one step at a time, please? Who's speaking, please?*

Jo: *Oh, sorry. My name's Jo Clarke. That's Jo without an 'e', and Clarke with one.*

Pat: *Fine. And you're calling from?*

Jo: *Top Fit Studios, Southport.*

Pat: *Okay, I've got that. Now, you're ringing about an enquiry, right?*

Jo: *Right. I'm calling about our enquiry for digital pulse counters.*

Pat: *Can you give me the details, please? I need the date, reference number, if any, and if possible the catalogue number, okay?*

Jo: *Sure. The date's the twenty-frst of October. The reference number's JC/2110/PC, and the catalogue number is DPC- 4X.*

Pat: *Okay, I've got that. Now, what's the trouble exactly?*

Jo: *Well, we still haven't received your offer,and things are getting a bit urgent this end. We already have several orders ourselves.*

Pat: *Oh, dear. Something's gone wrong here, I'm afraid. Could you hold on a moment, please? (pause) Hello?*

Jo: *Hello.*

Pat: *Well, I can't understand it.This offer went out by post on the twenty-fifth of October. You should have got it, well,a week ago.*

Jo: *Oh, the post again. Great. Could you do me a favour? Could you fax us a copy?*

Pat: *Of course. What's the number? It'llsave me...*

Jo: *Sure. 01714 for Southport, then 996603, okay?*

Pat: *Fine. 01714, then 996603, right?*

Jo: *That's right. Oh, and I don't want to put you under pressure but could you do that very soon?*

Pat: *Don't worry. I'll do it immediately.*

Jo: *Great. Bye now.*

Pat: *Bye.*

8 Unit 6 Exercise C4

Schmieder: *Good morning Mr Wilcox.This is Marc Schmieder. I hear you came back from Glasgow yesterday. Did you have a good trip?*

Wilcox: *Hello Herr Schmieder. Thank you. Yes, I did. I had a very useful talk with jeremy Scott of Strathclyde Engineering Ltd about your company's offers for machine tools. I'm almost sure he'll order several types of your machines. We also got a number of new orders, too.*

Schmieder: *I'm pleased to hear that.*

Wilcox: *Yeah, we are as well. There is one problem though. And that's the value of the euro.*

Schmieder: *What do you mean?*

Wilcox: *Well, you see, with the euro going up against the pound, your machines are getting expensive for the British market.*

Schmieder: *Mmh. I see. And what would you suggest our company should do?*

Wilcox: *Well, one solution would be to send your invoices in pounds, of course. Otherwise, you could lower your prices a bit or let us have more generous payment terms. That would also help to keep prices down.*

Schmieder: *Well, to be quite honest,Idon't think the management would agree to invoicing in pounds as it would put the entire risk on us. But I'll let my boss know about your suggestion concerning payment terms and get back to you. We certainly don't want to lose the British market now that things are beginning to look up.*

Wilcox: *I'm glad you understand our problem. And I shall be looking forward to hearing from you. Prices are very important to our customers. I'll also fax the new orders within the next couple of days.*

Schmieder: *Ok, thanks. So I'll get back to you as soon as I can.*

Wilcox: *That's fine. Bye for now.*

Schmieder: *Bye.*

9 Unit 7 Exercise C6

Conversation 1

Cunningham: *Good morning.This is Mr Cunningham from Atlanta Exports and Imports. Is Ms Kourgialis in?*

Secretary: *I'm sorry. Ms Kourgialis has gone out to see a customer. She's just rung to say she won't be back in today. Can I take a message?*

Cunningham: *Yes, thank you. That would be very kind. Would you just tell her that I phoned and ask her to call me back as soon as possible, please?*

Secretary: *I'm sorry. Could you just give me your name and your company again, please? I'll make sure Ms Kourgialls gets* *the message as soon as she comes in again tomorrow.*

Cunningham: *That would be fine. Thank you. So, my name is Cunningham. I'll spell it for you: C-U-N-N-I-N-G-H-A-M. And I'm phoning on behalf of Atlanta Exports and Imports Inc. Ms Kourgialis has got the number.*

Secretary: *OK, that's fine then. Thank you, Mr Cunningham. I'll pass on your message as soon as I can.*

Cunningham: *Good. Thank you very much for your help.*

<u>**Conversation 2**</u>

Kaurgialis: *Good morning, Mr Cunningham. You tried to reach me yesterday. I m sorry I wasn't in but I had to go out and see a customer.*

Cunningham: *Nice of you to call me back so quickly. My boss, Ms Smith, asked me to phone about the order we placed for an important customer of ours. She says they are in urgent need of the parts they ordered.*

Kourgialis: *I know what you are talking about. I did tell her before that there's been some trouble with this order.*

Cunningham: *Well, let me see now. Your manufacturers quoted delivery at the beginning of July. That's right, isn't it?*

Kourgialis: *That's right.*

Cunningham: *But the day before yesterday we were told that the equipment can't be delivered until mid- August at the earliest. In the meantime, however, my principal has opened the letter of credit as agreed.*

Kourgialis: *I'm very sorry there's going to be a delay but there's very little I can do. You see, I phoned the manufacturers this morning. And they've promised to dispatch the equipment in the second week of August.*

Cunningham: *The point is that work on the construction site could be seriously delayed. Ms Smith suggested you could perhaps get your manufacturer to ship at least part of the consignment in July?*

Kourgialis: *Well, you know, two units are in fact ready for dispatch. But the letter of credit says partial deliveries are not allowed.*

Cunningham: *We'll talk to the principal, Mr Moss, again. If he agrees that the two units should be dispatched now, we can change the letter of credit accordingly.*

Kourgialis: *I'm sorry about that. But I'm afraid, that's all we can do at present.*

Cunningham: *Well, I'll phone you again as soon as I know what's happening.*

Kourgialis: *OK, you do that. And I'm sorry I can't help any further.*

(10) Unit 8 Exercise C6

Loewe: *Guten Morgen.Fischer KG. Loewe am Apparat.*
Matthews: *Hello, Mr Loewe. Ms Matthews here from Barnes & Hopkins.*
Loewe: *Good morning. I hope you enjoyed the nice weather at the weekend.*
Matthews: *Yes, thank you. I hope you did, too. Any way, I have a little problem that I hope you can help me with.*
Loewe: *Oh dear. What's the problem?*
Matthews: *Well, your last invoice doesn't seem to make sense. It's invoice no. 23678 of 29 March.*
Loewe: *OK. Let me find that on my computer... Here we are. Number 23678 of 29 March?*
Matthews: *Yes, that's it. Well, you see, the quantities listed in the invoice don't tally with those on your packing list. The quantities you sent us were perfectly correct and matched your packing list. So, that part is OK. But on the invoice they are all different.*
Loewe: *Hmm.That shouldn't happen with our computer system because invoices are automatically generated at the same time as the packing lists. I don't understand that.*
Matthews: *Some of the prices are also a bit different and we normally get a cash discount but it isn't there.*
Loewe: *Really strange. Let's just check the customer number. What does it say on your copy of the invoice?*
Matthews: *It says: 453...Hey, wait a minute. That's not our number.*
Loewe: *Well, there must have been some mix-up with another customer. I'll ask accounts to look into it and get back to you later. Is that OK?*
Matthews: *Yeah, that's fine with me. Thank you very much.*
Loewe: *You're welcome. Bye now.*
Matthews: *Bye.*

(11) Unit 9 Exercise C5

Helen: *Hello. Is that Katja speaking?*
Katja: *Yes, that's right. Hello.*
Helen: *Hi, it's Helen Charlton. I've been trying to get hold ofyou for a while. It can be quite difficult because of the 7 hours time difference between here in Chicago and Germany.*
Katja: *Well, you got through in the end. What's the problem, Helen?*
Helen: *Well, we seem to be having some problems with your last consignment and your invoice. And I thought we'd better sort that out over the phone.*

Katja: *Sorry to hear that. But as you say, it's easier on the phone. Could you just give me the order number and the invoice number so that I can find the details, please?*

Helen: *Fine. The order number is 5566/A2.*

Katja: *That's 5566/A2.*

Helen: *That's it. And the invoice number is 293847/05, date: 4 March.*

Katja: *So, the invoice number again: 293847/05, date: 4 March...*

Helen: *Right. You see, we have problems with items 2 and 19.*

Katja: *Oh, I'm sorry. Let's take one item at a time.*

Helen: *Okay. So, item 2. We ordered 50 copies but you only sent us 15.*

Katja: *Fine. So we need to send you 35 more then.*

Helen: *That's right. Then there is item 19. Here you invoiced more copies than we actually received. You delivered 100 copies but you invoiced us for 150.*

Katja: *Well, there's something very badly wrong here. I'm very sorry. These are things that shouldn't really happen. Is that all, Helen?*

Helen: *Yes, that's all.*

Katja: *Well, I'll certainly ask someone to correct the invoice and cancel the one you've got straightaway. And then I'll send those 35 copies out to you today. But they will take a few days to get to you. Is that OK?*

Helen: *That's fine. The main thing is we receive them fairly soon because we've got orders for them.*

Katja: *Yeah, sure. I'm really very sorry about this.*

Helen: *Don't worry too much. Enjoy the rest of the day.*

Katja: *You too. Thank you. Goodbye.*

(12) Unit 10 Exercise C7

Sheila: *Bath 243987.*

MsBryant: *This is Liz Bryant from Hunters Ltd in Weston-super-Mare. Is that Mrs Anderson?*

Sheila: *No, sorry. This is Sheila Anderson. I'm the daughter actually. Can I take a message?*

Ms Bryant: *Well...If your brother is in, I would like to speak to him if I may.*

Sheila: *Well, my brother Roger is out all day. And I don't know when he'll be back. Can I take a message?*

Ms Bryant: *Thank you, yes, that would be kind. You see, your brother applied for a job with us.*

Sheila: *Yes, I know.*

Ms Bryant: *And I wanted to ask him... Well, you see he's been short-listed. And I would really like to arrange an interview, if possible.*

Sheila: *Well,that's good news. He'll be delighted.*

Ms Bryant: *We'll be interviewing candidates all day next week on Friday. And I had provisionally put his name down for 3 p. m. If that's OK?*

Sheila: *OK. So, it's Friday at 3 p. m. And where is the interview going to be?*

Ms Bryant: *We'll be interviewing in the Bristol Crown Hotel to make it easier for candidates. Our office in Weston-super-Mare is difficult to get to. Would you tell your brother, please. And also tell him that if the date and time are not convenient to ring me as soon as possible?If he can make it ask him to report to Reception. They will direct him.*

Sheila: *Of course, I will. Let me just repeat. So, you want to interview Roger next week on Friday at 3 p. m. And Roger is to report to Reception. They will direct him. And he is to phone you when he can't make it.*

MsBryant: *That's right. And I'll give you my telephone number. The area code is 01934, and the number is 453 2001. 2001 is my extension. And my name is Liz Bryant.*

Sheila: *I think I've got that.*

Ms Bryant: *Good, and thank you. Bye.*

Sheila: *Bye. And thanks for the good news.*

Packing containers and materials

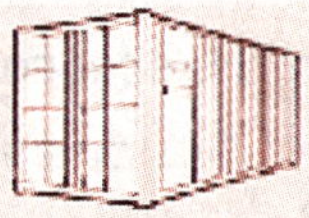

container

wooden crate

case

barrel

bale

drum

jar

carboy

bag

sack

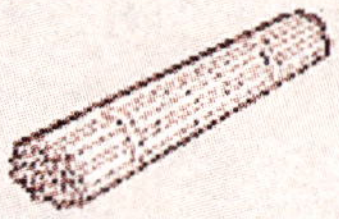

bundle

pallet

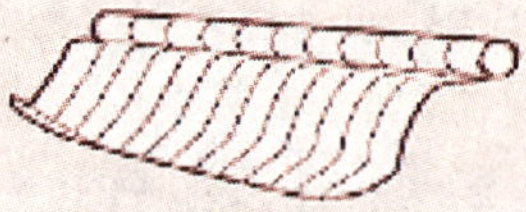

wrapping paper

corrugated cardboard

Answer Key

Unit 1 Form and layout of business letters

page 2

A Model letter

a

1 False.The letter is from Ahrens & Kessler and is to Robert Carr & Co Ltd in Bradford.
2 True.
3 Not enough information. It says she works in purchasing but it doesn't say if she is the manager or not.
4 Not enough information. It doesn't say how many colours the brochure is in.
5 False. They are particularly interested in the Carlton range of waxed coats and jackets.
6 True.

b

1 h 2 j 3 c 4 k 5 b
6 a 7 g 8 d 9 f 10 i 11 e

c

1 Good morning 2 you'll
3 attached PDF document
4 we're 5 seller
6 advert 7 we'd be glad
8 let us have 9 latest
10 We're especially keen on
11 Thanks a lot 12 Best wishes

page 9

C Practising language

1

1 blind carbon copy/blind copy circulated
2 carbon copy/copy circulated
3 company 4 electronic mail
5 enclosure 6 enclosures
7 facsimile message 8 limited
9 telephone

2

a The street number is in the wrong place: it should be '47 Rose Lane'.
The postcode should be on a separate line to the city.
b You don't need a comma after the street number.
The state should come before the ZIP code, i.e. 'Dallas TX 67432'.
c You don't need a point after the 'Ltd' in British firms.
The postcode should be on the same line as 'London' in London addresses.
d You don't need a comma at the end of a line.
'Scotland' should come after the postcode.
e You don't need a comma at the end of a line.
The town and the ZIP code should be on the same line.

3

1 25 April 1992; the twenty-fifth of April, nineteen hundred (and) ninety two
2 7 December 2000; the seventh of December, two thousand
3 15 February 2002; the fifteenth of February, two thousand (and) two
4 5 March 2003; the fifth of March, two thousand (and) three
5 10 August 1938; the tenth of August, nineteen hundred (and) thirty eight
6 31 October 2001; the thirty-first of October, two thousand (and) one

4

1 3 November 2000

2 5 January 2001
3 9 August 2002
4 8 May 2003

page 11

5

1 c/d   2 a   3 d   4 b

6

(a) Ahrens&Kessler GmbH
Dieselstraβe 24
D-28217 Bremen
(b) 4 February 20..
(j) Your ref: KF/sl
(k) Our ref: JB/bb
(h) Your enquiry of 16 February
(d) Dear Ms Feldman
(m) Thank you very much for your enquiry of 26 January.
We are happy to send you the catalogues and price-lists you asked for, including details of our Carlton range of waxed outer clothing.
We hope that you find our products of interest and would be delighted to hear from you again.
(l) Yours sincerely
(e) *Ranchit Patel*
(i) Ranchit Patel
(g) European Sales
(c) cc: John Garner, Export Planning
(f) Encs: catalogue (3x), price-list (3x)

Unit 2 Office communication: telephoning

page 13

A Taking notes

1a

1 Sam Kavanagh is calling.
2 He would like to speak to Ms Bach.
3 He would like her to ask Ms Bach to ring him back.
4 The caller's phone number is 00353 91 572231.
5 The message is urgent because Mr Kavanagh is away for the rest of the week.

b

1 'You' is Sam and 'me' is lisa.
2 'That's' is the spelling, 'we' is people in general and 'them' are the letters G and H.
3 'She' is Ms Bach and 'I' is Lisa.
4 'You' is Lisa and 'me' is Sam.
5 'You' is Lisa, 'her' is Ms Bach and 'it' is what he wants to talk about.
6 'I' is Lisa, 'she' is Ms Bach and 'your' refers to Sam.

page 14

2a

2 meeting   3 Sportmode
4 month   5 9:30
6 February   7 8
8 floor   9 conference centre
10 Theresienhöhe

b

1 for   2 at[1], in[2], in[3]   3 on[1], of[2]
4 in[1], for[2]   5 near[1], to[2]   6 in[1], on[2], of[3]

page 19

C Practising language

1

1 airlines   2 broadcasters
3 manufacturers   4 international organisations

page 20

6

1 b	**2** a	**3** b	**4** a
5 a	**6** b	**7** a	**8** b

G Good afternoon. Smith and Co. *How may I help you?* (1a)

J Good afternoon. Can I speak to Mr Smith, please?

G *May I ask who's speaking, please?* (3a)

J It's Julia Gordon from Kramer Ltd.

G *I'll just put you through,* Ms Gordon. (4b)

S Good afternoon. Mr Smith's office. Sarah Jones speaking.

J Hello. This is Julia Gordon from Kramer Ltd. Is Mr Smith there, please?

S *I'm afraid Mr Smith is busy at the moment.* (6a), But he should be free at about 3 o'clock. *Would you like to leave a message?* (8a)

J Could you tell him I called and *I'll ring again tomorrow,* please? (7b)

S Of course. Bye.

J Goodbye.

Unit 3 Office communication: emails

page 22

A Model emails

1a

1 The email is from Julia Graf to Joe Davis. It was sent on Wednesday 8 May at 14.56.

2 Mr Schubert is travelling to England by car through the Channel Tunnel.

3 Mr Schubert wants to visit Ashford on his first or last day because it is only 20 km from the Channel Tunnel.

4 Julia asks what Ms Medway would like to discuss at the meeting.

b

1 Not enough information. The email just says that Kate is busy all morning.

2 True.

3 False. Kate says Mr Schubert should come at about 10 am.

4 False. Kate and Mr Schubert could perhaps have lunch at the Old Mill.

5 Not enough information. The email only says that they could possibly go there for lunch.

6 Not enough information. The email only says that she wants to discuss problems with the cases.

c

1 10.30[1], 10[2], Ashford[3], Oxford[4]

2 Mr Schubert[1], volume[2]

3 Julia[1], ten[2], system[3], discount[4]

page 23

2

1g Before closing, Joe told the hotel to contact him if there were any queries.

2j He agreed with the hotel that the invoice would be sent to him at Kent Casings.

3e Joe asked for a full breakfast to be included in the price of the room.

4d Joe Davis sent an email to The Garden House on 14 May.

5a Joe had telephoned the hotel reception earlier on the same morning.

6i Joe told the hotel that the guest would also require off-road parking.

7f The purpose of the email was to confirm a telephone reservation.

8c The reservation was for a single room for one night for Rolf Schubert.

(Not used: b, h)

page 24

3

1 That's very generous of you.

2 I am now wondering whether you would like to join me for dinner.
3 I'm looking forward to it.
4 Many thanks for your kind invitation.
5 I'm delighted to accept.
6 I hope you'll let me return your generosity in the autumn.

page 30

C Practising language

1

1 Good morning	**8** won't arrive
2 change	**9** train
3 made	**10** until 10:50
4 going	**11** your trouble
5 be taken	**12** in touch
6 reservation	**13** questions
7 are	**14** regards

(Not used: arrive, tomorrow)

2

1 letter's	**6** don't[1], you'll[2]
2 name's[1], I'm[2]	**7** We'd[1], didn't[2]
3 She's	**8** haven't[1], isn't[2]
4 weren't	**9** mustn't
5 They'll[1], they're[2]	**10** I've[1], won't[2]

C Practising language

3

1 let you know	**11** okay
2 plans to visit	**12** could
3 fixing	**13** best
4 travel plans are	**14** things are
5 more or less	**15** getting
6 leaving	**16** an early
7 going to	**17** Thank you very much
8 flies back	**18** trouble
9 As	**19** let us know
10 wondering	**20** questions

4

(b) Good afternoon
(g) This is to confirm the phone reservation I made this morning.
(c) I'd like to reserve a single room with ensuite facilities for two nights, as follows:
(f) Guest Ms Birgit Klein
Arrival 06 June 20..
Departure 08 June 20..
(a) I also wish to book a space in the hotel garage. Ms Klein's car is a VW Passat, registration number EN-UU 107.
(e) Please note that Ms Klein won't arrive at the hotel before about 10.30 pm on 6 June.
(h) Thank you for your trouble, and please get in touch with me if you have any questions.
(d) Best regards

page 32

5

1 broken hinges—I PC plastic	**2** March
3 10—80,000—month	**4** increase—May
5 19—twice/double	**6** 3—B—middle

Listening comprehension

6

Name (Company/Person): Star Car Hire/Kim Cameron
Pick up date/place: 9am, Monday 16 March, Aberdeen Dyce airport
Return date/place: 6pm, Friday 20 March, Glasgow airport
Type of car: Peugeot 307 (Group C)
Price: £211.99
Extra details: Petrol not included. Give car back with full tank of petrol to avoid surcharge. Price includes full insurance and unlimited mileage.

<u>Email</u>

Hi Kate

I phoned Star Car Hire at Aberdeen Dyce about hiring a car for your holiday and spoke to somebody called Kim Cameron. She told me that it'll be quite okay to pick up the car at Dyce and return it at Glasgow.

Anyhow, I got a quotation for a Peugeot 307 from 9 am on Monday, 16 March to 6 pm on Friday, 20 March at a cost of £211.99. You get the car with a full tank, but you have to return it with a full tank, too. If you don't fill up the tank yourself, there is a £10 surcharge in addition to the cost of the petrol.

I asked about the price, which seemed a bit high, but Ms Cameron said that it includes full insurance and unlimited mileage, so there is no mileage surcharge.

Should I go ahead and make a firm reservation? (The office at Dyce is open until 10 pm, by the way.)
Joe

Unit 4 Enquiries

page 35

A Model phone call, fax and letter

1a

1 Adams **2** Pia Marx
3 export **4** Dorn
5 denim[1], jeans[2]
6 light stretch[1], colours[2]
7 samples[1], Italian[2]
8 standard collection

b

1 Yes, he does. **2** No, she doesn't.
3 Yes, it is. **4** Yes, she does.
5 No, it's not. **6** Yes, it can.
7 No, she doesn't. **8** Yes, she will.

c

1 Do you speak English?
2 Who would you like to speak to?
3 Who do you work for?
4 What are Style 4 looking for?
5 What are you manufacturing at the moment?
6 What do you want the denim for?
7 In what colours can Textil Dorn supply denim material?
8 Why is Mr Dorn faxing the details?

page 36

2

1 No, they aren't. **2** No, she doesn't.
3 No, they haven't. **4** No, she doesn't.

page 37

3

1 f **2** g **3** h **4** d
5 b **6** e **7** a **8** c

page 41

C Practising language

1

2 company **12** samples
3 manufacture **13** testing purposes
4 clothing **14** interested
5 retail outlets **15** trade discounts
6 address **16** trouble
7 edition **17** information
8 suppliers **18** enclosing
9 zip-fasteners **19** brochure
10 fashion **20** faithfully
11 grateful
(Not used: buyers, sale, sincerely)

2

2 selection **9** willing
3 samples **10** special
4 enclose **11** regular
5 latest **12** queries
6 current **13** contact
7 discounts **14** sincerely
8 volume

page 42

3

1 l	2 i	3 h	4 c	5 m
6 g	7 a	8 n	9 f	10 b
11 j	12 e	13 o	14 k	15 d

4

(b) Dear Sir or Madam

(f) We saw your advertisement in the July issue of 'Fashion World' and were particularly interested by your range of sportswear.

(a) As a supplier of tennis equipment and clothing, we are currently expanding our range and wish to start supplying women's wear as well as men's wear.

(j) We would, therefore, be very grateful if you could send us a copy of your brochure, as well as an up-to-date price-list.

(h) We would also appreciate information about volume and trade discounts.

(d) Thank you in advance for your help.

(e) We look forward to hearing from you soon.

(g) Yours faithfully

(i) Karen McDonald

(c) Purchasing Manager

page 43

D Writing letters

Dear Sir or Madam

We saw your advertisement in the latest edition of 'Health and Fitness World' magazine and would be interested to hear more about the products you advertise there.

We are a German fitness-centre chain based in Munich with branches throughout the country. As we are currently re-equipping some of our older centres, we are particularly interested in your ProMedic exercise bicycles.

We would be grateful if you could arrange for a representative to call on us here in Munich. We would also be grateful if you could send us your current price-lists and terms of business. In regard to this, we would particularly appreciate information about discounts for volume orders.

Thank you for your trouble, and we look forward to hearing from you in due course.

Yours faithfully

Unit 5 Offers and quotations

page 49

C Practising language

1

2 enquiry	12 cash discount
3 discounts	13 settlement
4 grant	14 weeks
5 trade	15 invoice
6 orders	16 interest
7 customers	17 hesitate
8 volume	18 further
9 excess	19 look forward
10 depending	20 receiving
11 pleased	

(Not used: business, fortnight, reminder)

2

1 enquiry	11 value
2 pleased	12 amount
3 offer	13 willing
4 note	14 settlement
5 delivery	15 receipt
6 stores	16 goods
7 confirm	17 immediately
8 offer	18 receipt
9 discount	19 satisfied
10 repeat	20 business

page 50

3

1 on	5 to

2 in... with
3 about
4 to
6 for
7 to
8 under

4

1 Why were the goods late?
2 Who did you speak to when you rang the firm?
3 How many CD burners have they placed an order for?
4 How can you place an order?
5 What was the enquiry for?
6 Where is the new delivery?
7 How did you send the offer?
8 Who dealt with Ajax's complaint?

Listening comprehension

5

Call taken by: Pat King, Sales
Time/Date: 11:12, 4 NOV 20..
Call from: Top Fit Studios, Southport
Caller: Jo Clarke
Subject: Enquiry Of 21 Oct, Ref JC/2110/PC
Product: Digital pulse counter, Cat No DPC-4X
Action agreed: Copy of offer will be sent out immediately per fax, number 01714 996603
Action by: self
Initials: PK

page 51

D Writing letters

Drechsler Freizeitaüsrustung GmbH
Harkortstraβe 22-24
58544 Witten
Phone (0 23 02)18 18-0 Fax (0 23 02)18 18 17
Internet www.dfza.de E-Mail info@dfza.de

Medway Outdoor Ltd
24 Riverside Road
Rochester, Kent
ME37HS
10 March 20..

Dear Ms Sutton

Your enquiry about sleeping bags

Thank you for your enquiry about lightweight sleeping bags of 5 March 20..

We are happy to send you the following offer for sleeping bags:

50 (fifty) Polar Star sleeping bags, Model PSLW—2,€ 75 each	€ 3,750.00
35 (thirty-five) South Pole sleeping bags, Model SPLW—4,€ 104 each	€ 3,640.00
Total	€ 7,390.00

Please note that all prices include delivery to your stores in Rochester.

We are pleased to give a trade discount of 15% and an additional cash discount of 2% for payment in full within 15 days of delivery.

The consignment will be dispatched by road within three working days on receipt of order.

We are certain that you will be completely satisfied with the quality and price of our products, and would be delighted to receive an order from you.

Yours sincerely
Drechsler Freizeitausrtistüng GmbH
Jessica Neuhaus
Jessica Neuhaus
EU Sales

Unit 6 Orders and acknowledgements

page 54

A Model letters

1

1 In view of the forthcoming Christmas break
2 your prompt reply
3 for delivery to be made
4 revised the quantities
5 Please note
6 We accept the prices and terms as stated in your offer

page 55

2

1 This may well be the case, the letter is written on 13 October but previous communication was written on 3 and 10 October.
2 Three signed copies are attached. Only the changes have to be authorised by signing next to them.
3 (correct)
4 Henderson Engineering Ltd requested three signed copies of the contract on 3 October.
5 Amendments to the contract were made in an exchange of faxes.
6 (correct)
7 The changes made mainly concern prices and terms of payment.
8 The changes need to be approved by signing next to them.
9 One copy is to be returned to the sender.
10 The goods should be ready for dispatch as agreed.

page 58

C Practising language

1

grant	a discount
reserve	the right
agree	to the terms and conditions
examine	the samples
guarantee	delivery
meet	the requirements
supply	from stock
place	an order

2

1 We feel that
2 If you do not
3 volume
4 expect delivery to be made
5 is due—receipt of invoice
6 a fortnight
7 warranty
8 Please let us know—dispatch

(Not used: kindly accept, order volume, we reserve the right to)

3

1 Thank you for your offer of 2 March which reached us today.
2 Having examined your samples, we are pleased to state that your goods meet our requirements.
3 However, your prices are too high for the market in which we operate.
4 Unless you can lower your prices or grant us more favourable discounts, we are unable to accept your offer.
5 Our order is placed on condition that the goods are delivered by 15 April at the latest.
6 We thank you for your order which will have our immediate attention.
7 We acknowledge your order of 22 February and accept your request for payment within 30 days net.
8 Please note that substandard goods will be returned at your cost and risk.

page 59

Role Play

5

B Good morning, Henderson Garden Centres, Claire Winterson speaking. Can I help you?

A Good morning. This is Rolf Schmidt from Bäumer & Winter in Balingen. We met at the trade fair. I hope it went well for you.

B Yes, thanks. We were pleased with the business we did.

A I'm glad to hear that. And thank you for the prompt reply to our enquiry. We really liked the designs and workmanship of the garden furniture you were displaying at the fair.

B I'm pleased to hear it.

A However, your prices are unfortunately a little

higher than those of your competitors.

B Oh, really. What do you think we should do about it?

A Well, we were wondering if the terms and prices could be improved?

B Hmm. To be honest, I think the prices are fair when you consider the quality and workmanship. What would the possible order volume be?

A We do have a large number of outlets, more than 30 garden centres in south and central Germany in fact, so it's likely to be quite high.

B Could I ask you to be more specific?

A Well, the initial order could be in the range of € 25,000 with further orders to be expected.

B In that case, we would be prepared to allow an additional volume discount of 5%. We could then review the terms for follow-up orders.

A Well, that would be okay for the first order but we'd hope for more generous discounts in the future.

B Okay then. Thank you for the order. I'll confirm the new terms in writing for you. I hope you'll be pleased with the goods. Bye for now.

A Thank you. Goodbye.

page 61

D Writing Letters

1

Hortex Gartencenter
Sebastian-Rieger-Str.42
68163 Mannheim
Tel.: 0621/363940-0 Fax:0621/363940-22
Email: info@hortex-gartencenter.de
Internet: www.hortex-gartencenter.de

West Sussex Garden Company
297 Willingdon Road
Hastings
East Sussex
TN35 6RS

13 August 20..

Dear Mr Snowdon

our order no. 05-3665

Thank you for your letter/fax of 6 August. We are pleased to note your improved volume discount and payment terms.

We are confident we will attract even more buyer interest with these lower prices. Please find our revised order for sunshades with stands in different designs and colour schemes and patterns enclosed.

We would like you to confirm that you can still supply the goods by the date originally agreed.

Thank you again for improving your terms and we look forward to receiving the goods in due course.

Yours sincerely

Kathrin Held

Kathrin Held (Ms)

Sales Assistant

Enc revised order no. 05-3665/2

page 62

2

Dear Mr McDougal

Thank you for your fax which we have just received. We are sorry to have to inform you that, unfortunately, Herr Wortmann fell ill immediately after his return from Ireland and is likely to be absent from work for some time. This is why not all the matters have been dealt with promptly, as is the policy of our company. We apologise most sincerely for failing to confirm your order and sending the documentation as promised by Herr Wortmann. But we are sure you will understand the situation. We will come back to you as soon as possible. Thank very much for sending the order copy which will make it much easier for us to deal with the matter. We promise to contact you as soon as possible. And once again thank you for your understanding.

Yours sincerely

Unit 7 Dealing with orders

page 64

A Model letters

2a

1 Order number 1186/27 is for tartan fabrics.
2 The order was due to be delivered by the beginning of August.
3 The buyer had advised his customers that delivery would be made by the beginning of August.
4 The buyer says that delays are sometimes unforeseen and unavoidable.
5 The customer wasn't informed of the delay.
6 New fabric arrived on 24 August.
7 The letter dated 24 August is signed by Ms Soames.
8 The tartan materials were slightly off-shade.

b

1 to promise shipment
2 to advise a customer
3 to hear from somebody
4 to acknowledge the receipt of a letter
5 to apologise for a delay
6 to begin manufacturing
7 to deliver an order
8 to cause serious trouble

page 66

3

1 What was the order for?
2 When can delivery be made?
3 Why are the goods palletised?
4 Who will be responsible for transport?
5 What will the hauliers do?
6 What will they issue?
7 Where is the invoice for the goods?
8 When do they expect settlement of the invoice?

page 69

C Practising language

1

1 order for	**7** you will realise
2 are pleased	**8** be fair to
3 we are sorry	**9** deal with orders
4 due to	**10** keep you informed
5 delay in delivery	**11** At this stage
6 everything we can	**12** apologise for

(Not used: process your order, unfortunately)

2

1 regret not being able
2 apologise/are sorry
3 apologise/am sorry for giving
4 excuse
5 am sorry/apologise for not having told
6 offer our apologies/apologise
7 excuse
8 regret having caused/are sorry/apologise for having caused

page 70

3

1 stipulated	**5** instructions
2 agreed	**6** adhered to
3 delivery	**7** contact you
4 receipt	**8** shipping

Listening Comprehension

4

1 He works for Atlanta Exports and Imports.
2 She has gone to see a customer.
3 No, she will not be back in today.
4 She took the message that Mr Cunningham had phoned and that Ms Kourgialis is to phone him as soon as she comes in tomorrow.
5 Yes, she does.
6 She wasn't in because she had to see a

customer.

7 Delivery was promised at the beginning of July.

8 Delivery will be made in mid-August at the earliest.

9 The problem is that work on the construction site could be seriously delayed.

10 He suggests that the manufacturer makes a part shipment in July.

Memo

I spoke to Ms. Kourgialis this morning about the urgency ofour order. She informed me that their manufacturer cannot supply the equipment before mid-August. I made clear that the delay in delivery might affect our L/C and also delay work on the construction site. We agreed that we will both explore the possibility of a part delivery. That would mean changing the L/C however. I'll contact her again shortly.

page 71

D Writing letters

1

Kunststoffe Röhncke & Meueler GmbH
Schweriner Str. 67
18069 Rostock
Telephone (0381) 80045 66
Fax (03 81) 8 00 45 10
Email info@roehncke-meueler.de
Internet www.roehncke-meueler.de

Barksdale Cases Ltd
Unit K4
Troon Way Business Centre
Humberstone Lane
Leicester
LE4 9AH

13 February 20..

Dear Mr Sherratt

Your order for vinyl

Thank you for your order Of 2 February. You will be pleased to learn that all the items ordered can be shipped except for item No. 17F. Due to an unexpectedly high demand, this item is temporarily out of stock in the colour and material you require.

As new supplies are expected within a fortnight, we would suggest that we hold your order until then. Of course, we could dispatch the availble goods immediately and send the remainder as soon as new supplies have come in.

We apologise for the inconvenience and look forward to receiving your instructions by return.

Yours sincerely

page 72

2

Melchers & Schmitt GmbH & Co KG
Fabrikzeile
95028 Hof

Derby Warehousing Ltd
12-14 Leicester Street
Derby DE5 9BN
Fax No. 01332-75764-500

(Date)

FAX MESSAGE

Dear Mr Fisher

Your order for shelving system Orion

Thank you for order of... for the supply and installation of a complete shelving system for your warehouse.

We are sorry to have to inform you today that the delivery of the shelving material will be delayed by approximately two weeks. This is (entirely) due to supply problems of one of our sub-suppliers, for which we are not to blame. We were informed that important input materials were not available in time for production. Considering the current level of production we foresee that the assembly of the system can start at the beginning of June.

You may rest assured that we will do everything in our power to speed up production and have already taken steps to reorganise our production process accordingly. We are currently drawing up a revised schedule and

will let you have detailed information in the next few days.
Once again we offer our apologies for this delay which is beyond our control.
Yours sincerely

Unit 8 Payments and reminders

page 75

A Model letters

3a

1 consignment
2 invoice
3 remittance
4 overdue
5 disregarded—outstanding
6 appreciate—possible
7 by return
8 settlement
9 immediate attention
10 solicitor

b

1 They bought video tapes.
2 The number was 5421/05.
3 The invoice amount is £2,004.50.
4 The invoice was due for payment by approximately 20 May.
5 Payment was due within a fortnight from the date of invoice.
6 About 10 weeks have passed.
7 About 14 weeks have passed.
8 The customer is given 10 days to pay.

page 79

4

a We refer to
b (we) apologise most sincerely
c in clearing our account
d reminders
e it certainly is not our practice to
f settling your account
g out of business
h obligations
i problematic business climate
j our efforts
k remainder
l are making every effort
m as soon
n Sincerely yours

page 81

C Practising language

1

1 for	6 to	11 of
2 of	7 on	12 by
3 for	8 of	13 of
4 in	9 In	14 to
5 of	10 for	15 from

2

1g As requested we have credited your account with the amount of $756.00.
2e Despite our repeated request for payment, we have received neither your payment nor an explanation for your failure to clear your account.
3 —
4h We are pleased to confirm that the payment of £1,275.69 clears your account.
5b We request payment of the invoice total by 25 October.
6d Our invoice no. 5647G is still unpaid.
7a Your account still shows a debit balance of € 12,375.00.
8c We must now insist on immediate settlement of our invoice.
9 —
10f If we do not receive your remittance by 16 February, we shall have to consider taking legal steps.

page 82

3

(c) Dear Mr Raumer

(f) Two months ago we supplied you with a variety of buttons for the tourist trade in your region.

(i) We went out of our way to ensure that the goods reached you promptly in time for the beginning of the tourist season.

(e) Therefore, we are all the more surprised and disappointed to find that you do not seem willing to fulfil your obligations.

(g) We wrote to you asking for payment three weeks ago.

(b) But so far we have neither received payment nor did we have a letter explaining the reasons for the delay in settling our invoice.

(l) You will understand that the products in question are low-margin articles.

(a) Any further delay in payment would wipe out our small profit altogether.

(k) We would like to ask you to give this matter your immediate attention and clear your account promptly.

(d) We have enclosed a copy of our invoice for your information.

(h) We look forward to hearing from you by return.

(m) Yours sincerely

(Q) Claire Williams

page 83

Role Play

5

B Guten Morgen.Textil Dorn.Pia Marx am Apparat. Was kann ich für Sie tun?

A Good morning. This is Jane Adams from Style Four. I'm calling because of your latest invoice. There are problems with several items.

B I'm sorry about that. Could you give me the order number and date?

A Of course. It's 13 January and the number is 5378/P.

B Okay... Right, I've got it up on my screen. Which items are wrong?

A There are problems with items 2, 5 and 8.

B What's the problem exactly?

A Well, the invoice price for item 2 seems to be higher than list price. The invoiced quantity for item 5 is wrong. It says 52 but it should have been 25. And item 8 was on special offer but the invoice price is identical to the list price.

B Oh, I'm sorry about that. I'll talk to the sales department about that.

A That's okay. When do you think can I expect a reply?

B I'll contact sales at once. I think typing mistakes are probably the problem. I'll hopefully ring you back today.

A Thank you. It would be good if everything could be put right as quickly as possible.

B Of course. My apologies once again.

page 84

D Writing letters

1

Dear Mr/Ms...

We refer to our statement of... for the first quarter which we sent you about four weeks ago. So far, both your account statement from early April and also our reminder have gone unanswered. We must ask you now to settle the outstanding amount of £25,374.75 without delay.

Should you wish to discuss other possibilities of clearing your account, we would be open to consider your suggestions.

If payment has already been made, please disregard this letter. We look forward to hearing from you by return.

Yours sincerely

2

Wegener Kunststofftechnik GmbH
Wendenstr.87
31226 Peine

Beattie Engineering Ltd
24-26 Duncan Street
Sheffield S5 6DK
England
(Date)
Dear Ms Greer
Invoice NO. 24680
Thank you for your letter of 20 September. We are sorry to note that you had reason to remind concerning the settlement of your am. invoice.
Unfortunately, we had some problems in our accounts department which have come to our notice only recently. As a result, some invoices were not processed in a proper manner. In the meantime, we have dealt with the problems.
All outstanding invoices have been cleared and I am pleased to assure you that we had already instructed our bankers to remit the outstanding amount in full before your letter arrived.
We apologise most sincerely for the inconvenience our delay in payment may have caused you and thank you for your patience.
Yours sincerely,

Unit 9 Complaints

page 87

A Model letters

1

1 The consignment arrived yesterday.
2 The colours of some of the material did not quite match those of the samples.
3 Ms Adams complains about order numbers 4673 and 4679.
4 Ms Adams asks for replacements for items 8 and 10 to be sent immediately if the wrong material was sent.
5 Items 8 and 10 will be held until the problem has been solved.
6 Ms Adams intends to settle the invoice when the matter has been resolved.

page 92

C Practising language

1

1 We **are afraid** you **sent** us the wrong goods.
2 The contents of case 7 **do not agree** with the packing list.
3 We **had ordered** 500 sweaters, but only **received** 250.
4 When we **checked** the consignment, we **found / noticed** that the jeans were of the wrong sizes.
5 Unfortunately, the material **does not match** the samples.
6 When we **opened** the case, we **found/ noticed** that item 6 from our order **was missing.**
7 Some of the china **was broken** because the goods **were not packed** sufficiently well.
8 We **see** no alternative but to **return** the goods to you.
9 Please **ensure** that the replacement goods **arrive** in time for the fair.
10 You **will understand** that the delay in delivery **has caused** us considerable inconvenience.
(Not used: be damaged, complain, pay)

2

1d We accept responsibility for the damage which must have occurred in transit.
2b We are prepared to keep the goods at a substantially reduced price.
3i Your failure to supply the goods on time has caused us considerable inconvenience with our customers.
4a Unfortunately, we have reason to complain about a delay in delivery.
5g We have to ask for compensation to cover our losses.
6f We offer our sincere apologies for this error.
7c In the circumstances, we are, of course,

prepared to replace the goods at our expense.

8h We suggest that you report the matter to your insurance company.

(Not used: e, j)

page 93

3

1 On examining the articles, we discovered that some of them were damp.

2 After operating the machine for a short time, we noticed that it did not perform as expected.

3 For your information, please find some photos enclosed as proof of the damage.

4 It goes without saying that we cannot offer goods of this quality to our customers.

5 We have no alternative but to delay payment until the replacement goods have arrived.

6 In the circumstances, we have decided to return the faulty goods at your risk and expense.

7 We must therefore ask you to let us know what can be done to put the matter right.

8 We will only be prepared to keep the goods if you reduce the price by at least 20 per cent.

4

As you can see from the charts, the number of complaints received per 1,000 orders has decreased again since reaching a high point in 2001. However, although the number of complaints decreased between 2001 and 2002, the number of customers who said they were dissatisfied stayed at about the same level while the number of those who were very satisfied even decreased almost by half. In spit of the high numbers of satisfied customers has consistently remained roughly the same.

page 94

Listening comprehension

5

Dear Helen

Thank you for your phone call this morning. I'm very sorry about the things that went wrong with this order. In the meantime, I sent memos round to the departments concerned. I asked dispatch to ship 35 copies of item 2 from your order no. 5566/A2. And I also asked the accounts department to correct item 19 where we invoiced 150 pieces instead of the 100 that you actually received. Accounts will send you an amended invoice. I'm sorry once again for these mistakes and hope you will receive the missing items and also the amended invoice soon.

Best wishes

Katja

page 94

D Writing letters

1

Our order no. 1357/TS—Complaint about faulty consignment

Dear Mr Bulmer

We have received the goods from our order no. 1357/TS yesterday. On unpacking the goods we noticed, however, that some of the plastic foil and cardboard covering was damaged and torn. Some of the washing machines were so badly scratched that we will have to return them to you as they are of no use to us. As this incident is somewhat unusual, we have enclosed some photos as proof.

We would like to ask you to investigate the matter and you may very well wish to take this up with the shipping company.

You will understand that we have no use for the machines which are scratched and would ask you to send us replacements straightaway. This is particularly urgent as we have firm orders for all of your washing machines. A detailed list of the damaged items is enclosed.

We are sorry to have to report this to you and trust you will send us a full report once you have investigated this matter.
We look forward to hearing from you.
Yours sincerely

page 95

2

Dear Ms Solms
Thank you very much for your letter Of 20 June 20.. We are sorry to learn that our consignment of cotton shirts gave reason to complain. You can be assured that we take every possible care when packing our goods. After taking up the matter with our dispatch department, I can confirm that the boxes of this consignment contained 500 shirts each as stated in the packing list and also in our invoice. The cartons were in perfect order when they left our premises. We always seal our cardboard containers with hard-wearing printed tape. Furthermore, our forwarder has confirmed receipt of your consignment in perfect order and condition. Therefore we are at a loss to understand how this could have happened. We will certainly look into the matter and hope to be able to report back to you soon.
As regards the missing shirts, please indicate the sizes of shirts that you want replaced by return. If necessary, we can send these shirts by express to ensure that they reach you as soon as possible.
Once again we are sorry about this incident and thank you for reporting the matter to us.
We look forward to hearing from you shortly.
Yours sincerely

3

Dear Joanne
Thank you for your mail. I'm sorry to learn that your consignment of leather belts (your order no. 7788-DA) didn't turn out to your satisfaction. As Sylvia is away on a three-day business trip, I've been asked to deal with the matter. I have asked our colleagues in the dispatch department to look into the matter. I hope to have their findings later today and will come back to you then. I hope you will understand that I cannot be more specific at this stage. But I can assure you that we will be dealing with your complaint promptly and thank you for your patience.
I'll contact you again later today when I have the results of our investigation. Then we can decide what needs to be done.
Kind regards

Dear Joanne
I refer to my mail earlier today. I'm sorry to report that a mistake has occurred at our dispatch department. We found that you have, in fact, received the wrong consignment. As you will no doubt have realised, the packing list you received with your consignment corresponds entirely with your order but the quantities sent do not. I apologise for this mistake most sincerely. We have already dispatched the missing goods by express and the consignment should reach you in about two days.
We kindly ask you to return the wrong consignment to us carriage forward. Of course, we will also refund any other expenses you may incur.
Once again, we are very sorry about this and hope you will accept our apologies.
Yours sincerely

Unit 10 Applying for a job

page 99

A Model letters and CVs

1

1 They are expected to do a work placement abroad.

2 Timo is planning to go to Britain for three months.
3 Timo did a vocational training.
4 Timo is now a fully qualiried Management Assistant in Wholesale and Foreign Trade.
5 Timo's command of English is good and he also knows some Business English.
6 Timo is planning to come to Britain from 1 July to 30 September.

page 104

C Practising language

1

1c stockist
2a accounts manager
3d warehouse manager
4a advertising agent
5a deputy manager
6a builder

2

1 advertisement	9 standard
2 issue	10 continued
3 a candidate	11 challenging
4 believe	12 helpful
5 completing	13 testimonials
6 department	14 available
7 activities	15 interview
8 customers	

(Not used: experience, interest, references, training)

page 105

C Practising language

3

1 I have trained with Wolters Maschinenbau GmbH as a management assistant in human resources.
2 I worked as an assistant to the area sales manager in Swansea for two years.
3 During my training as a management assistant in insurance, I attended additional courses to improve my computing skills.
4 I will complete my training as a management assistant in property management in two months' time.
5 Since leaving school, I have worked as a temp in the logistics department of IPEX Mediatechnik GmbH.
6 My training as a management assistant in wholesaling and retailing lasted three years.
7 Having completed my training in office communication, I am looking for an opening in an engineering company.
8 After my traineeship with Steinmeyer & Partners, I continued to work in the capacity of field representative with this company.

4

1 The advertisement on your website for the post of bilingual sales manager interested me.
2 I am interested in applying for the advertised vacancy and enclose my personal profile.
3 As an experienced administrative assistant, I am confident I will / I hope to meet your requirements.
4 I believe that I have the necessary drive and team spirit to contribute to the business success of your company.
5 My present job involves a lot of keyboarding activities. Therefore, I am familiar with the standard word processing software.
6 Having gained experience in a small but busy office, I am now seeking a new challenge.
7 I feel that, with my foreign language skills, I can contribute to your international sales efforts.
8 I would welcome the opportunity to come for an interview.
9 Should you require any further information, please phone or mail me at any time.
10 If necessary I can supply references (from my former employers).

5

Application for post of senior secretary/PA

It was with great interest that I read your advertisement for the post of senior secretary/PA in yesterday's issue of the *New York Times.*/ Your advertisement for the post of ...in yesterday's... interested me very much.

Therefore, please find enclosed an application for the position advertised./Therefore I would like to apply for the advertised post and have enclosed my application.

Having recently graduated from Albany Secretarial College, I am.../Having recently completed my education at..., I am confident...

In addition to good key boarding skills (50 wpm), I also have some shorthand skills (40 wpm).

In the position of secretary at Ogilvy& Partners, I gained some experience in working in a law firm and copy-typing.

Now I am seeking a new challenge in an office with... /Working in an office...will be a new (and exciting) challenge.

In addition/Furthermore, I would also like to make better use of my foreign language skills which I have acquired at school and in evening classes.

The standard software programs are well known to me.

Becoming part of... environment is something I would very much enjoy/enjoy very much.

If you require any supplementary information, I will be happy to supply this and I am available for an interview at any time.

You can contact me by phone or email./Contact can be made by phone...

page 108

D Writing letters and CVs

1

1 [a] advertisement; [b] post, position; [c] wish, would like; [d] be considered

2 [a] see; [b] CV, profile, resume; [c] necessary, required; [d] qualifications; [e] requirements

3 [a] attending,leaving; [b] college, university, the polytechnic; [c] trained as

4 [a] gained; [b]experience; [c] agency, company; [d] to get to know; [e] work; [f] department, office

5 [a] If,Should; [b] additional, further, more; [c] call, contact

2

Dear Mr Henderson,

(g) I found your address in the career centre's job file and wish to apply for the advertised post of junior office assistant.

(b) I will have completed my two-year training as an office assistant with Hunters Corp here in Portland by the end of June.

(c) But as my company has no opening for me, I am now exploring opportunities to use my skills elsewhere.

(e) You will see from my resume and certificates that I have already gained some work experience in the sector in which you operate.

(d) During my traineeship, I also attended evening classes in office management, computing and general secretarial duties.

(f) I am confident that my training and the skills I acquired at college make me suitable for such a position.

(j) I hope to gain further experience and to make a positive contribution to the success of your business.

(i) If you require any additional information, please do not hesitate to contact me by phone or mail.

(a) An interview can be arranged at anytime.

(h) I look forward to hearing from you.

Yours truly,

page 109

3

(see page 152)

4

Points to consider when doing this exercise:

Executive assistant

Skills and qualifications: experience as secretary /personal assistant for heads of department, able to work under pressure, friendly personality, selfstarting qualities, ability to run the office, well educated, good qualifications, foreign languages, PC skills, good references

Legal assistant

Skills and qualifications: experience as secretary /personal assistant, able to work under pressure, good language skills, efficient worker, friendly personality, well educated, good qualifications, PC skills, good keyboarding skills, good references

Bilingual secretary

Skills and qualifications: experience as secretary, able to work under pressure, good keyboarding skills, good language skills (near-native in two languages, advanced in a third), efficient worker, friendly personality, well educated, good qualifica-tions, PC skills, good references

Receptionist

Skills and qualifications: experience as receptionist/telephonist, good communicative skills, some knowledge in a foreign language, will undertake office work if required, efficient, friendly personality, neat appearance, good references

Christina Voigt
Robert-Koch-Str. 15
80021 Munich
Tel. 089/495 08 19
E-Mail: tinavoigt@t-online.de

CURRICULUM VITAE

Personal data	Born on 21 November 1984 in Kempten Female Single	
Education	1990—1993	Primary School in Munich
	1993—2002	Grammar school in Munich, Abitur (average grade 2.3)
	1999—2000	6 months exchange visit to Seaford sixth form college
Work experience	July 2001	1 month’s work experience at Barclay’s Bank London—customer services department
	2002—present	Traineeship at Hypo-und Vereinsbank (HVB) in Munich
Activities and interests	Languages	English—fluent French—fairly fluent
	Computer literacy	Famitiar with standard software programs
	Interests	Reading, riding, travelling, meeting people

References supplied upon request